BRITAIN'S RAILWAYS BY NIGHT

Previous page:
A chilling winter mist begins to gather at Derby on 20th February 1985 and accentuates the effect of the headlight on Brush Class 47/4 No. 47608, awaiting a path into the station platforms with a rake of Travelling Post Office vehicles.
Camera: Nikon FM2, film rating: 400ASA
Exposure: 30secs @ f4

Colin Marsden

The Brush Class 89 Co-Co electric locomotive No. 89001 rests inside its home depot of Bounds Green on the night of 30th August 1988. Before dawn rises on the following morning, the locomotive will haul empty coaching stock (ecs) to Peterborough where, at the time of this photograph, it was booked to haul the 07.16 weekday HST commuter service from there to King's Cross and the 17.36 evening return.
Camera: Nikon FM2, film rating: 400ASA
Exposure: 5secs @ f8

Brian Morrison

BRITAIN'S RAILWAYS BY NIGHT

Colin J. Marsden & Brian Morrison

Oxford Publishing Co.

Previous page:
Under the yard lights at Bristol Bath Road depot during the 'GWR 150' celebrations on 28th October 1985 are 'Manor' class 4-6-0 No. 7819 *Hinton Manor* and 'King' class 4-6-0 No. 6000 *King George V* with a Class 56 diesel, No. 56031 *Merehead,* just visible in the background.
Camera: Mamiya 645, film rating: 200ASA
Exposure: 45secs @ f8

Graham Scott-Lowe

Bristol Temple Meads station at 20.04 on a cold 11th January 1983. Brush Class 47/0 No. 47069 is on the left with the Penzance-Glasgow parcels train and No. 47203, of the same type, on the right with another parcels service from Bristol to Paddington. Much more film is expended on night photography during the winter months due to shorter daylight hours permitting an earlier start to activities.
Camera: Bronica EC, film rating: 400ASA
Exposure: 40secs @ f8

Brian Morrison

A FOULIS-OPC Railway Book

© 1989 B. Morrison, C.J. Marsden
& Haynes Publishing Group

British Library Cataloguing in Publication Data
Morrison, Brian
   Britain's railways by night.
   1. Photography. Special subjects. Railways.
Manuals

I. Title   II. Marsden, C.J. (Colin J)
778.9'49385
ISBN 0-86093-431-4

Library of Congress catalog card number
89-84717

Published by:
Haynes Publishing Group
Sparkford, Near Yeovil, Somerset. BA22 7JJ

Haynes Publications Inc.
861 Lawrence Drive, Newbury Park, California 91320, USA.

Printed by: J.H. Haynes & Co. Ltd

Contents

	Page		Page
Introduction	6	Newspaper Traffic	78
Night Photography	7	Whistling in the Dark	82
Steam by Night		A.C. Electrics	84
London in the 1950s	8	Two's Company	87
Bristol Temple Meads in the 1960s	13	Deltics	88
Around London – Waterloo	16	North of the Border	90
– Paddington	19	Action in a Flash	94
– King's Cross	22	Preston Vespers	97
– Liverpool Street	24	Departmental	98
London's Midland Termini		Where it is Always Night!	100
– Euston	26	Inclement Weather	102
– St Pancras	28	Night People	105
– Marylebone	30	Southern Outskirts	106
On Depot	32	Signals and Signal Boxes	108
Night Mail	39	Nightfall in the West Country	110
Marshalling Yards	44	Docklands in the Dark	112
– and Terminals	45	The Ubiquitous Class 31	113
Bristol Temple Meads in the 1980s	46	Salisbury After Sunset	116
After Hours at the 'Plant'	49	Bumps in the Night	118
Nocturnal Freight	50	Steam Preservation	120
'Sleepers'	54	The End	128
Class 71s at Victoria	57		
Granite City after Dark	58		
Night Pilots	60		
Derby Nights	62		
'Westerns' and a 'Warship'	64		
Night Parcels	66		
Evening Off Peak – Provincial Sector	70		
– and Network SouthEast	74		

At St Pancras station on the night of 21st November 1985, Class 317/1 emu No. 317308 forms the 22.18 for Bedford Midland and Class 47/4 No. 47491 *Horwich Enterprise* heads the 22.25 TPO for Newcastle. Reflections from a wet platform enhance the attractiveness of the scene.
Camera: Nikon FM2, film rating: 400ASA
Exposure: 20secs @ f5.6

Brian Morrison

Introduction

For the majority, railway observance is a pursuit carried out during daylight hours and people often seem surprised to find that, in most areas, railway activity carries on right through the night! Indeed, at some locations, traffic flows are more prolific through the dark hours than in the daylight ones. This title has been prepared to illustrate the varied and abundant railway operations which are not usually seen by the casual observer.

Most regions operate night passenger services on selected routes, principally of inner-city and InterCity variety with the Provincial Sector being something of a poor relation. The London Midland, Western and Scottish Regions operate nightly sleeping car services which radiate from London to Cornwall, North East England, and South Scotland and even the Southern Region has one 'sleeper' service from Poole to Edinburgh. Today these trains are formed of the latest Mk 3 stock which provides the overnight traveller with accommodation equivalent to that of a good, if small, hotel room. Sleeper services depart late evening at around 20.00-23.00 enabling a destination arrival between 05.30-08.30 on the following morning, with passengers permitted to 'lay in' on the early arrivals until around 07.30. In addition to overnight sleeping car services, a number of conventionally-formed overnight trains operate on the InterCity Sector and on the London-Scotland route. These are operated under the 'Nightrider' trade name and formed of Mk 2 stock with subdued lighting. In a number of inner-city areas, particularly around London, all-night services operate on suburban routes with trains being made up of conventional unit formations.

One of the foremost users of the night network is the Royal Mail for transportation of both letter and parcel post. In many areas, covering all five regions, special Travelling Post Offices (TPOs) are operated. These are formed of special TPO stowage and sorting vehicles which enable post to be sorted en route by Post Office staff and off-loaded at specified points for collection by local Post Office personnel. Apart from the TPOs, a considerable amount of mail and parcels is also carried by normal service trains, with sealed mail bags being loaded and collected by Post Office staff on a timetabled basis. In some areas passenger stock, when not required for normal duties, is utilised to carry Post Office cargo.

Another night contract which the railways retained for very many years was the conveyance of newspapers from the major printing cities of London, Manchester and Glasgow to the provinces. The products of all printing houses were loaded onto a common train where distribution, sorting and packing for various wholesalers was accomplished by special packing staff. For these services British Rail operated fleets of BG, GUV and PVG vans which were dedicated entirely for newspaper usage. From 1988, however, politics within the newspaper industry coupled with new premises and new technology brought about the transfer of all national newspaper distribution to the roads, leaving only a few magazines and the like to be transported by rail in the old time-honoured style.

BR's Railfreight Sector takes advantage of the slack night hours to operate a number of its timetabled Speedlink freight services which virtually link every part of the railway network. In general terms, the Speedlink trains depart from railheads or private sidings in the early evening and arrive at the terminal or transfer point by early the following morning.

Civil Engineering departments also take advantage of the general reduction in rail traffic during the night period by carrying out maintenance work. This may well entail taking complete possession of individual lines after the last timetabled train has passed through and returning the line for operational purposes prior to the first working of the following day; in some circumstances the 'possession' being temporarily lifted to enable a special train to pass which cannot be diverted from its booked route.

Motive power and vehicle maintenance is carried out on a large scale during the night hours. Usually locomotives, and particularly InterCity 125 units, arrive at their servicing depots around midnight and in under six hours have to be ready for the road again. During this time a complete technical inspection takes place with brake block/pad changes if required, plus cleaning and repairing of passenger accommodation. All the large diesel multiple unit (DMU) and electric multiple unit (EMU) servicing depots, such as Ilford and East Wimbledon, have a number of night staff employed on carrying out service checks and programmed maintenance after the stock arrives 'home' following the daylight operations.

In addition to covering the modern traction scene on Britain's railways by night, this title also contains examples of steam traction at night taken during the 1950s and 1960s when running regular BR services, plus examples of the current steam preservation scene around the country after dark.

The authors of this book – the first of its kind to be devoted entirely to railway operations and photography at night – trust that the reader will find the contents helpful in the understanding of railway operations after dark and that the explanations of photographic technique will prove helpful. In this respect our sincere thanks go to the many railway photographers who have supplied material for the illustrations and divulged some of their individual photographic secrets. Thanks also go to the many railway staff who have assisted while photographs were being taken, to Derek Mercer for his expert printing of all the authors' own work within these 128 pages and to Nikon (UK) Ltd who kindly provided the loan of a special and very valuable Nikon Nocturne lens, with which a number of our illustrations were taken.

Brian Morrison
& Colin Marsden

Night Photography

Often train movements which occur during the night are of more interest than daytime ones. More freight rumbles through, special engineering workings operate, Travelling Post Offices can be observed and sleeping cars abound. Many other types of working can also be seen during the hours of darkness and in many instances they can be recorded on film regardless of the absence of natural light.

Apart from the obvious camera loaded with film, the basic requirements for the night-time photographer are a sturdy tripod, a cable release, a torch and some warm clothing; even in the summer months, station platforms and the like can be quite chilly during the 'small hours'. Special permission is not normally needed for taking photographs from a station platform providing that one is in possession of a valid ticket for travel or a platform ticket. However, ensure that your presence does not in any way hinder the day-to-day tasks of railway staff and your venture should go well. If you do encounter liverish, unreasonable and generally miserable night staff or the like, the best advice is to move on. Most railwaymen are pleased that some people show an interest in their job, whereas a minority seem to be of the opinion that they are operating some form of secret government establishment where no one shall enter!

Assuming that all is well, place the camera firmly on the tripod and attach the cable release, set the shutter speed and lens aperture with the aid of the torch (if you have a modern camera with LED readout in the pentaprism, this piece of equipment will have less use), find your subject matter and you are ready for your first night railway photograph. What shutter speed and lens aperture do you use? As a general rule, something around f4 to f5.6 is recommended for a start and the exposure time should be gauged in seconds rather than a small fraction of a second. Stations, yards etc., all vary with regard to light intensity and some experimentation is advisable before embarking upon a long session. Throughout this album, the camera exposure details are shown below each photograph and some idea of a starting point will soon become apparent.

The 15.10 Waterloo-Exeter St Davids train draws to a halt at Salisbury station on 28th November 1981 powered by English Electric Class 50 No. 50035 *Ark Royal*. With prior permission from the driver, a combination of a very short time exposure plus flash was used to obtain this result.
Camera: Nikon FE, film rating: 400ASA
Exposure: 1/15th sec @ f2 + flash

Brian Morrison

A flash gun can be an asset at night but should always be used with absolute discretion. Other than with special permission and prior warning to the train crew, a flash gun should never be fired at a moving train as temporary blindness could result in these circumstances and a signal could be unseen with tragic consequences. Where flash is particularly useful is in providing some illumination to part of a subject which is in complete darkness or even providing the means of taking a photograph when the subject matter is completely in the dark without illumination of any kind at all, such as beneath a bridge. Some examples of this technique can be found within these pages and the method employed is described.

One other handy accessory is a piece of matt black card. Often during a lengthy time exposure with the camera shutter open, something occurs which is not wanted to register on the film; movement of another train in the background or adjacent platform, the appearance of someone walking up the platform towards the camera, a platform trolley on the move, etc. Any of these will appear as a blur on the film but can be avoided by covering the open lens with the card, thus interrupting the exposure until the movement has passed or ceased.

Expensive photographic equipment is not a necessity for night photography and even modest cameras and lenses can give excellent results, providing they have a time exposure capability. Why not try your hand at this quite fascinating part of the photographic art? Exposure latitude is far greater than during the daylight hours and in many ways allows for greater control over the end result. Present day modern lighting usually provides a most acceptable level of illumination for picture making, and most of all, the activity can be great fun and the results often surprisingly good.

Steam at Night
London in the 1950s

On Sunday, 21st November 1952, an Adams, London & South Western Railway 0-6-0 of Class 0395, arrives at London Victoria with a Railway Correspondence & Travel Society special train which had travelled the Bisley branch earlier in the day.
Camera: Agfa Isolette, film rating: 200ASA
Exposure: 3mins @ f8

Brian Morrison

An evening train for Basingstoke awaits the scheduled departure time before steaming away from Waterloo station on 29th February 1952 behind Bulleid 'West Country' Pacific No. 34011 *Tavistock*. Station lighting in the 1950s was not nearly so bright as is the case today and a similar scene recorded here in the 1980s would need only one tenth of the exposure time which was necessary over thirty years ago.
Camera: Agfa Isolette, film rating: 200ASA
Exposure: 3mins @ f8

Brian Morrison

In the early 1950s, the regular 20.13 parcels train to Reading from Waterloo often came up with unusual motive power and this was certainly the case on 29th February 1952, with a Wainwright, South Eastern & Chatham Railway Class D 4-4-0 No. 31746 rostered for the turn. The grimy exterior of the engine was such as to eliminate any light reflection and the necessary exposure under the dim Waterloo lights of the day was appropriately a long one.

Camera: Agfa Isolette, film rating: 200ASA
Exposure: 4^1/2 mins @ f8

Brian Morrison

On the same crisp February evening in 1952, Drummond, London & South Western Railway Class T9 'Greyhound' 4-4-0 No. 30721 of Nine Elms shed, simmers at around 175lbs per square inch in readiness for its sortee into the night from Waterloo, with a parcels and newspaper train bound for Salisbury.

Camera: Agfa Isolette, film rating: 200ASA
Exposure: 3mins @ f8

Brian Morrison

The dim lighting of St Pancras station is made to appear reasonably bright by means of the time exposure. On 11th January 1952, Stanier 'Jubilee' Class 4-6-0 No. 45651 *Shovell* awaits the 'off' with the 20.10 departure for Derby.
Camera: Agfa Isolette, film rating: 200ASA
Exposure: 3mins @ f8

Brian Morrison

Opposite top:
On the same chill January night in 1952, an evening commuter train for Bedford waits to leave St Pancras station behind Fowler Class 4MT 2-6-4T No. 42334. The station light bulbs make a brave attempt to illuminate the scene through the smokey atmosphere prevailing and, again, the lack of reflection from the flanks of the engine has resulted in a lengthy exposure time being required.
Camera: Agfa Isolette, film rating: 200ASA
Exposure: 4mins @ f5.6

Brian Morrison

Opposite below:
On 10th April 1953, the precursor of the present day "Nightrider" service, the "Starlight Express", was introduced between London and Scotland giving cheap overnight travel for passengers who were prepared to 'rough it' a little and snatch what sleep was permissible, while sitting upright in an old carriage which was not well sprung by today's standards! Gresley Class A3 Pacific No. 60111 *Enterprise* was appropriately provided for the first run from Marleybone station to Glasgow St Enoch and, surprisingly, the event attracted far more enthusiasts than expected. No light whatsoever shone upon the engine that night and assistance from a large flash bulb was necessary for this result to be obtained.
Camera: Agfa Isolette, film rating: 200ASA
Exposure: 1/25th sec @ f4.5 with PF1 flash bulb

Brian Morrison

An evening stopping service for Baldock waits to leave the suburban platforms at King's Cross station in the winter of 1952, powered by Thompson Class L1 2-6-4T No. 67745 from Hitchin shed (34D). During the long exposure, the train guard deigned to stop in one position for rather too long and, in consequence, he has registered on the film as a 'ghost'. An example of where the exposure should have been interrupted until movement had ceased, but it was thought at the time that he would keep walking and not stay in the one position long enough to appear on the film.

Camera: Agfa Isolette, film rating: 200ASA
Exposure: 3mins @ f8

Brian Morrison

On the same winter evening, a relief to the famed "Aberdonian" express is about to move away from King's Cross station behind Class A3 Pacific No. 60112 *St Simon*. A small flash bulb was fired onto the front of the engine during the time exposure in an attempt to obtain a little detail in this unlit area which, otherwise, would have registered completely black. With hindsight, a larger flash bulb would have been more beneficial!

Camera: Agfa Isolette, film rating: 200ASA
Exposure: 3mins @ f8 with PF3 flash bulb

Brian Morrison

Bristol Temple Meads in the 1960s

▲

Beneath the roof of the old Brunel station at Bristol on 17th January 1964, 'Jubilee' class 4-6-0 No. 45612 *Jamaica* awaits departure time with an express parcels service for Leeds.
Camera: Voightlander Bessa, film rating: 100ASA
Exposure: 1¹/₂mins @ f8

David Nicholas

▼

Comparing this view of Temple Meads station with the one shown on page 4, very little appears to have changed in twenty years. On 13th November 1963, Collett 4900 class 'Hall' 4-6-0 No. 6955 *Lydcott Hall* prepares to depart with a local service heading in the direction of Swindon.
Camera: Voightlander Bessa, film rating: 100ASA
Exposure: 15secs @ f4.5

David Nicholas

With loading nearing completion, 'Jubilee' class 4-6-0 No. 45682 *Trafalgar* prepares to head away into the night with a parcels train on 27th January 1964.
Camera: Voightlander Bessa, film rating: 100ASA
Exposure: 1min @ f8

David Nicholas

With smokebox number removed but, happily, still having the cabside numbers and nameplates intact, 'Castle' class 4-6-0 No. 4089 *Donnington Castle* stands at Bristol Temple Meads station on 29th January 1964 with a haul of vans.
Camera: Voightlander Bessa, film rating: 100ASA
Exposure: 1¹/₂mins @ f5.6

David Nicholas

4900 class 'Hall' 4-6-0 No. 4993 *Dalton Hall* is ready to move fruit vans away from Bristol Goods on the same evening.
Camera: Voightlander Bessa, film rating: 100ASA
Exposure: 2mins @ f6.3

David Nicholas

On 15th November 1963 at Temple Meads station, 4900 class 'Hall' 4-6-0 No. 5900 *Hinderton Hall* prepares to move away southwards with the 19.00 Bristol-Weymouth semi-fast service. It is a pleasant thought that this scene could be recreated today as *Hinderton Hall* is one of the engines preserved in the care of the Great Western Society at Didcot.
Camera: Voightlander Bessa, film rating: 100ASA
Exposure: 1min @ f8

David Nicholas

Parcels are unloaded from a train of vans which has arrived at Temple Meads station on a particularly dark February night in 1964. Motive power for the journey has been provided throughout by 6959 class 'Modified Hall' 4-6-0 No. 6982 *Melmerby Hall*.
Camera: Voightlander Bessa, film rating: 100ASA
Exposure: 1^1/2mins @ f8

David Nicholas

Riddles BR Standard Class 9F 2-10-0 No. 92070 awaits a clear road through Temple Meads station on 14th November 1963 whilst hauling a westbound fitted freight.
Camera: Voightlander Bessa, film rating: 100ASA
Exposure: 2mins @ f6.3

David Nicholas

Around London – Waterloo

On the evening of 10th November 1988, the 20.45 service to Bournemouth and Weymouth awaits departure from Waterloo formed of Class 442 'Wessex Electric' unit No. 2407. Probably as a result of having a front end 'spoiler' and 'go-faster' stripe, these impressive-looking trains were quickly dubbed 'GTis' by the enthusiast fraternity!
Camera: Nikon FM2, film rating: 400ASA
Exposure: 1sec @ f5.6

Brian Morrison

Available to night travellers and among the Southern Region's fastest trains of the day, the 02.45 'Newspapers' from Waterloo to Bournemouth is seen at the London terminus on 7th October 1974 powered by Class 74 electro-diesel locomotive No. 74010. The station lighting stopped short of the locomotive and it was necessary to use electronic flash in order to illuminate it. The lighting on the station and coaches was successfully recorded with a time exposure while the 'flashing' was taking place. The Class 74s were withdrawn from service in December 1977.
Camera: Bronica S2a, film rating 400ASA
Exposure: 1¹/2mins @ f8 with multiple flash used on the locomotive only.

Brian Morrison

On the crisp, early morning of 30th March 1981, Birmingham RC&W Class 33/0 No. 33016 is in the process of having its train loaded with newspapers at Waterloo station prior to departure as the 01.40 for Yeovil.
Camera: Mamiya 645, film rating: 400ASA
Exposure: 15secs @ f5.6

Colin Marsden

Compare the present day lighting at Waterloo with that of some thirty years earlier as illustrated on page 9. The 06.12 departure for Windsor & Eton Riverside is stabled in platform 15 overnight and on 21st April 1981 is formed of a Class 405 4SUB emu No. 4657. With the exception of one working, preserved example, all of these 1949 vintage units have since been withdrawn from service. At the buffer-stops of platform 14 is Class 73/1 electro-diesel No. 73129, now named *City of Winchester*.
Camera: Mamiya 645, film rating: 400ASA
Exposure: 12secs @ f5.6

Colin Marsden

With headlight ablaze, Brush Class 47/4 No. 47587 is rostered for the last train of the day from Waterloo to Salisbury and awaits departure time of 22.10 before taking its rake of Network SouthEast liveried stock out into the night.
Camera: Nikon FM2, film rating: 400ASA
Exposure: 5secs @ f5.6

Brian Morrison

Three disparate front-ends at Waterloo station buffer-stops at one minute past midnight on 30th March 1981. From left to right, the emus are of Class 508, 405(4SUB) and 423(4VEP) respectively. All the Class 508 units were later transferred to Merseyside and replaced on Southern Region by Class 455.
Camera: Mamiya 645, film rating: 400ASA
Exposure: 20secs @ f8

Colin Marsden

With the time at exactly 19.12, the driver of the 19.12 Waterloo-Basingstoke service awaits the guard's signal prior to taking his charge away from Southern Region's principal London terminus, on 9th December 1981, for a journey with eight stops which is scheduled to take 1hr 3mins. The leading 4-car set is a Class 423(4VEP) emu No.7737.
Camera: Bronica EC, film rating: 400ASA
Exposure: 15secs @ f5.6

Brian Morrison

The great cathedral-like Brunel roof arches of Paddington station are best recorded after dark by means of a time exposure. On 19th April 1984, a parcels service for Birmingham is loaded at platform 1 while the locomotive for the journey, Class 47/0 No. 47144, has just backed onto the train.
Camera: Olympus OM2, film rating: 100ASA
Exposure: 30secs @ f8

Paul Shannon

Just why Western Region persist in applying set numbers to their allocated InterCity 125 power cars, and not the actual power car number in the manner of Eastern Region is not known, but it certainly produces the occasional smile when a scene such as this is recorded! At the Paddington buffer-stops on 30th January 1988, the 23.55 for Cardiff is on the right while its apparent twin on the left waits to leave for Old Oak Common depot with empty stock of an earlier arrival from Plymouth. These power cars are just two of four of the InterCity fleet fitted with Mirrlees engines in place of the original Paxman Valentas.
Camera: Canon EF, film rating: 400ASA
Exposure: 10secs @ f5.6

Ken Brunt

– Paddington

Ready for departure from Paddington station on 9th January 1988, the 23.15 overnight van train for Penzance is headed by English Electric Class 50 No. 50005 *Collingwood* which is painted in the revised Network SouthEast Sector livery which omits the original sharp upturn of colour at the front end of the locomotive, and also consists of a darker shade of blue.
Camera: Canon EF, film rating: 400ASA
Exposure: 10secs @ f5.6
Ken Brunt

The north side of Paddington station is utilised for the majority of the suburban services and the non-passenger workings, as witness this scene of Class 37 No. 37177 heading the 21.28 van train for Gloucester alongside a mail train, photographed on 17th October 1984.
Camera: Pentax 6x7, film rating: 400ASA
Exposure: 15secs @ f5.6
Colin Marsden

As darkness gathers at Paddington on 7th February 1985, the headlight beam of Class 50 No. 50002 *Superb* becomes more and more pronounced. Heading the 17.47 for Westbury, the 'Hoover' awaits a path into the night as the short time exposure records as a blur the exit of an InterCity 125 train from platform 5.
Camera: Nikon FM2, film rating: 400ASA
Exposure: 4secs @ f2.8

Brian Morrison

A shortage of available motive power at Old Oak Common depot on the same evening resulted in the utilisation of Class 47/4 No. 47628, despite the work on the locomotive in connection with 'GWR 150' events being incomplete. Painted in a form of GWR Brunswick lined green, but minus the brass numberplates and *Sir Daniel Gooch* nameplates, which had still to be fitted, but sporting tiny painted numbers, the locomotive comes to a halt at the Paddington buffer-stops with the 17.46 empty coaching stock working from Twyford.
Camera: Nikon FM2, film rating: 400ASA
Exposure: 4secs @ f2.8

Brian Morrison

Opposite top:

The changes which have taken place at King's Cross station during the past decade have all increased service efficiency but have been to the detriment of the railway photographer. Before the advent of overhead power lines and their ugly supports, and prior to 'rationalisation' of the station and lines, Class 55 'Deltic' No. 55001 *St Paddy* prepares to power north on 6th December 1974 with the 22.15 sleeping car service to Aberdeen, the "Night Aberdonian".
Camera: Bronica S2a, film rating: 400ASA
Exposure: 30secs @ f5.6

Brian Morrison

Opposite below:

At the King's Cross buffer stops at 05.40 on 27th June 1988, Class 90 electric locomotive No. 90005 *Financial Times* has arrived with a 'Type Trials' test train from Grantham, the stock of which includes sleeping cars. Following trials and evaluation, the Class 90s commenced working one passenger diagram from Euston in September 1988 followed by regular services in November. The very short camera exposure needed beneath the station lighting has enabled the crew member in the cab to be recorded without any apparent blurring as a result of movement.
Camera: Canon EF, film rating: 400ASA
Exposure: 2secs @ f2.8

Ken Brunt

Dead on time at 20.04, an InterCity 125 High Speed Train set with power car No. 43063 leading, is about to depart from King's Cross on 7th February 1985 forming the 20.04 service to Hull.
Camera: Nikon FM2, film rating: 400ASA
Exposure: 10secs @ f8

Colin Marsden

During the months of winter, 'night' photography is possible in the late afternoons. At King's Cross on 29th November 1987, Class 317/2 emus Nos 317365 and 317359 form the 17.15 to Welwyn Garden City and the 16.45 to Hertford North, respectively.
Camera: Canon EF, film rating: 400ASA
Exposure: 2secs @ f2.8

Ken Brunt

– Liverpool Street

At Liverpool Street station on 1st September 1985, the 23.00 service for Ipswich awaits departure time behind Class 86/2 electric locomotive No. 86246 *Royal Anglian Regiment* which is painted in the attractive livery of the InterCity Sector. During a period in 1988–89 this locomotive was part of the Railfreight Sector allocation and dedicated to the Freightliner division of Speedlink Distribution, being modified and classified 86/5, carrying Railfreight's double grey livery and the number 86505.
Camera: Mamiya 645, film rating: 400ASA
Exposure: 8secs @ f5.6

Brian Beer

A night scene with a difference. The oil lamp table at Liverpool Street station, with lamps prepared for the overnight newspaper and mail trains whch were scheduled for the night of 1st September 1985.
Camera: Mamiya 645, film speed: 400ASA
Exposure: 10secs @ f8

Brian Beer

On 25th February 1984, Class 47/4 No. 47583 *County of Hertfordshire* was used to haul in empty coaching stock to form the 17.35 service from Liverpool Street to Cambridge. After departure of the train, the locomotive, now released from the buffer stops, awaits to exit from the platform and perform its next duty.

Camera: Nikon FM2, film rating: 400ASA
Exposure: 1/200th @ f4 with electronic flash

Brian Morrison

London's Midland Termini – Euston

▲
The Class 370 Advanced Passenger Trains were first introduced in 1979 and each comprised six articulated trailer cars with one power car, and they carried set numbers 370001 to 370007. On 3rd March 1985, the latter stands at Euston station awaiting signals to proceed to Wembley depot after working a special 'Chartex' train. The APT programme was finally abandoned later that year and all the units have since been withdrawn following various periods in storage.
Camera: Canon FX, film rating: 400ASA
Exposure: 5secs @ f4

Ken Brunt

▼
The 01.10 Holyhead to Euston train, the famed "Irish Mail", stands at the London terminus in the 'small hours' of 14th December 1975 headed by Class 86/2 Bo-Bo electric No. 86257. In the years which have passed since this scene was recorded, the route indicator panels on the locomotive have been abolished and replaced with marker lights, the name *Snowdon* is now carried and InterCity Sector livery is sported.
Camera: Bromica S2a, film rating: 400ASA
Exposure: 15secs @ f8

Brian Morrison

Allocated to Railfreight Distribution for working Freightliner traffic, No. 86503 *City of Lancaster* has been suitably modified for such use and also repainted into sector colours of two-tone grey, but has yet to receive sub-sector colour decals. Allocated to Willesden depot, the locomotive was used for working ecs to form the 21.05 sleeping car service to Inverness on 25th February 1989, and is seen here at the Euston buffer-stops. The TOPS number carried when allocated to InterCity Sector was 86205 and was due to be reapplied in late 1989.
Camera: Nikon FM2, film rating: 400ASA
Exposure: ¹/₂sec @ f4

Brian Morrison

On the night of 16th November 1984, a Class 82 electric locomotive, No. 82008, waits to haul empty Mk 3 coaching stock away from Euston station to Willesden carriage sidings (now called Wembley InterCity Depot). All of the ten machines which made up Class 82 are now withdrawn from service.
Camera: Canon FX, film rating: 400ASA
Exposure: 20secs @ f5.6

Ken Brunt

▲ With the new St Pancras station clock clearly showing the time as 22.33, the 22.48 for Bedford Midland awaits custom on 21st November 1985, formed of Class 317/1 emu set No. 317341. In the opposite platform, the 23.05 vans train for Derby and Nottingham is in process of being loaded and will be powered by Class 31/1 No. 31250.
Camera: Nikon FM2, film rating: 200ASA
Exposure: 30secs @ f4

Brian Morrison

▼ Cardiff Canton-based Class 37/4 No. 37428 *David Lloyd George* awaits departure from St Pancras on 21st October 1988 heading the 18.20 InterCity service for Derby. This class of locomotive was surprisingly diagrammed for the train from the commencement of the 1988/89 Winter timetable but, in fact, worked the service only a few times before Class 47s took over.
Camera: Nikon FM2, film rating: 400ASA
Exposure: 5secs @ f5.6

Brian Morrison

Opposite top:
When high winds brought down the catenary on the West Coast Main Line on 14th January 1984, a number of interesting train substitutions took place. One of these was formed of Mk 3 coaches making up the 17.42 additional service from St Pancras with Class 25/2 Bo-Bo No. 25201 providing power to haul the train, but fitted for steam heating only, it was unable to heat the stock.
Camera: Olympus OM1, film rating: 400ASA
Exposure: 30secs @ f8

Michael J. Collins

Opposite below:
On the night of 8th September 1984, Class 40 1Co-Co1 No. 40122 (D200) is surprisingly rostered for the 00.20 newspaper train from St Pancras to Derby. Here, the train is shown waiting to leave the fine old Midland Railway train shed which looks a little bare without its usual massive station clock which was missing at the time, awaiting provision of the new one illustrated on the page opposite. Alongside the "Whistler" is a Class 317/1 emu No. 317345 forming the 00.45 to Bedford Midland.
Camera: Canon FX, film rating: 400ASA
Exposure: 5secs @ f4.5

Ken Brunt

– Marylebone

A somewhat ethereal view of the Marylebone train shed photographed on a wet November night in 1984. Soon to emerge from the station's dry interior, a Class 115 Driving Motor Brake Second (DMBS) leads a 4-car dmu which is shortly to depart for Aylesbury.

Camera: Mamiya 645, film rating: 400ASA
Exposure: 30secs @ f5.6

Brian Beer

As night falls on 3rd December 1984, 'push-pull' fitted BRC&W Class 33/1 Bo-Bo No. 33118 awaits departure from Marylebone station with a "Rail Ambassador" exhibition train.

Camera: Mamiya 645, film rating: 400ASA
Exposure: 1sec @ f4

Brian Beer

▲
Passengers on the 19.25 service for Banbury steam up the inside of the
windows of the Class 115 DMBS No. M51674 which will head the
train from Marylebone on the cold evening of 7th February 1985.
Camera: Nikon FM2, film rating: 400ASA
Exposure: 6secs @ f2.8

Brian Morrison

▼
On the same evening, another BR Derby Class 115 dmu, led by DMBS
No. M51900, waits to proceed to Marylebone depot for overnight
attention and stabling.
Camera: Nikon FM2, film rating: 400ASA
Exposure: 4secs @ f2.8

Brian Morrison

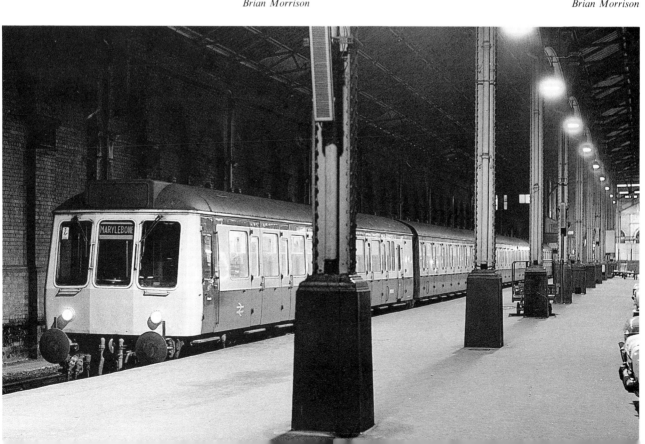

On Depot

Use of a 24mm wide-angle lens has enabled the fuel line in Buxton depot yard, and the two English Electric Class 20 Bo-Bos, Nos 20141 and 20195, stabled there on 21st February 1985, to remain sharply in focus.
Camera: Nikon FM2, film speed: 300ASA
Exposure: 30secs @ f5.6

Brian Morrison

Ready to be put to work on china clay haulage on the following morning, English Electric Class 50s Nos 50012 *Benbow* and 50045 *Achilles* peer out into the Cornish night from the confines of the old St Blazey steam shed on 18th February 1982. With the only light available to the camera coming from a few electric light bulbs within the building, the required exposure for this result was a long one and, in addition, multiple flash was used during the exposure time in order to illuminate the brickwork of the shed.
Camera: Bronica EC, film rating: 800ASA
Exposure: 1min @ f5.6 plus multiple flash

Brian Morrison

▲

Standing in the yards at London's Bounds Green depot on the night of 30th August 1988 are GEC Class 91 No. 91003 attached to a surrogate Driving Van Trailer (DVT), InterCity 125 power car No. 43063 and Class 47/4 No. 47660. The Class 91 locomotive is under test, the HST power car is awaiting attention within the depot and the Type 4 diesel is stabled until its next duty on the following morning.
Camera: Nikon FM2, film rating: 400ASA
Exposure: 20secs @ f5.6

Brian Morrison

▼

Motive power depots see the largest amount of activity during the night hours, when the traffic flows are at their lowest. This 15th December 1988 view of Laira depot shows Class 50 No. 50041 *Bulwark* in company with Class 47/4 No. 47508 *SS Great Britain* and Class 50 No. 50029 *Renown* outside the inspection shed awaiting a service check before resuming duty.
Camera: Nikon FM2, film rating: 400ASA
Exposure: 10secs @ f5.6

Colin Marsden

On a bitterly cold night in February 1983, Class 50 No. 50002 *Superb* stands in Saltley depot yard, Birmingham, adjacent to Class 47/0 · No. 47052 and an unidentified 'Peak'.
Camera: Nikon EM, film rating: 400ASA
Exposure: 8secs @ f11   *Don Gatehouse*

A nearby street lamp provides the only illumination for this pleasant line-up of motive power at Gloucester depot on 24th November 1983. From left to right are Class 47/0 No. 47239, Class 31/1 No. 31181, another Class 47/0, No. 47076, and a Class 119 power car belonging to dmu No. B591.
Camera: Canon AE1, film rating: 400ASA
Exposure: 30secs @ f8   *Michael Rhodes*

Class 47/0 No. 47109 and BRC&W Class 27/0 Bo-Bo No. 27045 while away the night inside Aberdeen Ferryhill depot on 14th November 1984. Both locomotives have since been withdrawn from service and Ferryhill is now closed.
Camera: Mamiya 645, film rating: 400ASA
Exposure: 4secs @ f5.6

Colin Marsden

A Class 08 shunter, No. 08141, stands alongside two newly delivered Electroputere Class 56s, Nos 56014 and 56015, inside Barrow Hill depot in 1977 prior to commissioning.
Camera: Canon AE1, film rating: 400ASA
Exposure: 6secs @ f8

Michael Rhodes

The yard lights at Buxton depot shine through a cold night mist and produce a rather unusual effect upon a BR Derby Class 108 dmu which has the Driving Motor Composite (DMC) No. M53932 facing the camera. Class 20 'Choppers' make up the majority of the other motive power which can be seen stabled here on the night of 21st February 1985.
Camera: Nikon FM2, film rating: 300ASA
Exposure: 15secs @ f4

Brian Morrison

With the Class 508 emus now working entirely around Merseyside and the Class 405 4SUBs having been withdrawn, this October 1980 scene inside Effingham Junction depot in Surrey of Nos 508009 and 4618 is now history.
Camera: Mamiya 645, film rating: 400ASA
Exposure: 8secs @ f8

Colin Marsden

Stabled at Exeter St Davids overnight on 5/6th November 1988, Railfreight Sector's Class 50/1 No. 50149 *Defiance* shares accommodation with standard Class 50 No. 50009 *Conqueror* and green-liveried Class 33/0 No. 33008 *Eastleigh*. *Defiance* has since been returned to standard operating condition, reverted to number 50049 and painted in Network SouthEast livery.
Camera: Nikon FM2, film rating: 400ASA
Exposure: 30secs @ f5.6

Colin Marsden

The lighting in Cornwall's St Blazey depot yard was just about sufficient for a long time exposure to be made in order to record Class 45/0 'Peak' No. 45002, stabled there overnight on 18/19th February 1982. The locomotive was withdrawn from service just over eighteen months later, in September 1984.
Camera: Bronica EC, film rating: 800ASA
Exposure: 1min @ f5.6

Brian Morrison

Brush Class 31/4 No. 31411 stands over an inspection pit inside the East London depot of Stratford on 16th January 1986. Introduced in March 1961, this locomotive was one of the first batch of 19 of the class to be fitted for electric train heating (eth) and despite having had a working life of over 25 years, has every chance of remaining in service for some years to come.
Camera: Nikon FM2, film rating: 400ASA
Exposure: electronic flash @ f5.6

Brian Morrison

Empty coaching stock workings for Euston InterCity services emanate from Wembley depot where the coaches are cleaned and serviced. Waiting to leave the yards on the misty evening of 8th Nobember 1988, three such trains are headed, respectively, by Class 87/0 No. 87001 *Royal Scot* and a pair of Class 85s, Nos 85030 and 85014.
Camera: Nikon FM2, film rating: 400ASA
Exposure: 10secs @ f8

Brian Morrison

Night Mail

On 1st December 1983, the 19.00 northbound TPO stands at Derby waiting to move off behind Class 45/1 'Peak' No. 45116.
Camera: Mamiya 645, film rating: 400ASA
Exposure: 10secs @ f5.6

Colin Marsden

A variety of locomotive types are rostered to work the various TPOs. Here, Eastleigh-based Class 33/0 No. 33020 finds itself at Cardiff station on 9th June 1982 providing power for the 21.25 Swansea-Bristol postal service.
Camera: Bronica EC, film rating: 400ASA
Exposure: 45secs @ f11

Brian Morrison

At Bristol Temple Meads station on 11th January 1983, mail is ready to load aboard the 19.57 service for Severn Beach, which is formed of a Pressed Steel Company Class 121 single-car unit from Plymouth Laira depot, No. P126. In reality, the unit consists solely of DMBS No. W55026.
Camera: Bronica EC, film rating: 400ASA
Exposure: 20secs @ f5.6

Brian Morrison

Southern Region emus are often used for postal traffic, both mail and parcels, with mailbags being loaded into stock which is normally used for passengers. One such turn was the 19.26 from Waterloo to Waterloo, via Kingston, shown here in the bay platform at Twickenham on a wet 6th October 1981 and formed of Class 405 'Mary' No. 4639, since withdrawn.
Camera: Mamiya 645, film rating: 400ASA
Exposure: 10secs @ f5.6

Colin Marsden

Even High Speed Train sets are not sacrosanct where the carriage of mail is concerned. On 21st November 1985, the luggage compartment of InterCity 125 power car No. 43085 *City of Bradford* is loaded at St Pancras station prior to its departure at the rear of the 23.20 service for Sheffield.
Camera: Nikon FM2, film speed: 300ASA
Exposure: 20secs @ f4

Brian Morrison

The Southern Region's small fleet of ten Class 419 Motor Luggage Vans are normally utilised attached to the front or rear of emus which form various boat trains to and from the Kent passenger ports of Folkestone and Dover. Being fitted with two 250hp English Electric traction motors, however, they are power cars in their own right and are quite capable of being run as single units or in multiple with one another. During the night of 10th November 1988, No. 9004 (68004), the first of the type to be painted into the red livery of the Post Office, forms a postal train at the Central Section buffer stops of London Bridge station and when loaded, will travel to Redhill.

Camera: Nikon FM2, film rating: 400ASA
Exposure: 15secs @ f8

Brian Morrison

The 22.48 service from St Pancras to Bedford Midland is a combined passenger and mail train. Formed of a Class 317/1 emu No. 317341, loading takes place on 21st November 1985 prior to departure.

Camera: Nikon FM2, film rating: 300ASA
Exposure: 20secs @ f4.5

Brian Morrison

Acting as station pilot at Exeter St Davids on 14th July 1983, Class 08, shunter No. 08954 is busily engaged attaching vans onto the rear of the Penzance-Paddington TPO.

Camera: Mamiya 645, film rating: 400ASA
Exposure: 6secs @ f5.6

Colin Marsden

At Newton Abbot station on 30th April 1981, the driver of Class 50 No. 50025 *Invincible* looks back along the train as Post Office staff load his charge, the 19.27 Penzance-Paddington TPO.
Camera: Praktisix II, film rating: 400ASA
Exposure: 5secs @ f8

Geoff Gillham

Mail is unloaded from the 17.07 Bedford-Derby van train following arrival at its destination on 20th February 1985. Class 31/4 A1A-A1A No. 31438 awaits completion of the task prior to moving the empty stock away to the sidings for the night. Before conversion for eth, this locomotive was classified as 31/1 and carried the number 31139.
Camera: Nikon FM2, film rating: 400ASA
Exposure: 6secs @ f2.8

Brian Morrison

As Class 47/4 No. 47419 draws the 17.53 Workington-Huddersfield TPO to a halt at Lancaster station's platform 5 on 8th February 1983, mail bags are ready for loading.
Camera: Nikon FM2, film rating: 400ASA
Exposure: 1min @ f8

Brian Morrison

On the following night, the same train utilises platform 4 at Lancaster station instead of platform 5 and an entirely different camera viewpoint is possible. The motive power on this occasion is another Class 47/4, No. 47455. The exposure required is greater than if the train had been photographed from the platform side as the available station light is weaker, being that much further away.
Camera: Nikon FM2, film rating: 400ASA
Exposure: 15secs @ f2.8

Brian Morrison

There are times during daylight hours when Temple Mills marshalling yards, in East London, appear rather run down and almost deserted. At night, however, the complex comes to life with arrivals and departures occurring frequently. On 18th October 1985, the 12.18 Dover-Tyne Yard 'Speedlink' freight prepares to continue its journey northwards behind Class 47/3 No. 47301, while Class 08 No. 08440 bustles about on a variety of shunting duties.
Camera: Nikon FM2, film rating: 300ASA
Exposure: 20secs @ f2.8

Brian Morrison

A view of Toton marshalling yards on a September night in 1981 with one of the many Class 20s which are allocated to Toton Traction Maintenance Depot (TMD), No. 20143, in view under the yard floodlights hauling a short rake of air-braked 'Railfreight' vans.
Camera: Pentax 35mm, film rating: 400ASA
Exposure: 15secs @ f2.8

Chris Davis

Class 47/0 No. 47264 leading Class 25/3 No. 25324 prepares to depart from Lawley Street terminal, Birmingham, on 25th November 1983 providing the equivalent of Type 6 power for the 19.15 'Freightliner' for Ipswich. As a large amount of their work is undertaken at night-time, lighting at Freightliner Terminals (FLTs) is always good.
Camera: Nikon FE, film rating: 400ASA
Exposure: 8secs @ f11

Don Gatehouse

On 18th October 1985, Class 47/4 No. 47596 *Aldeburgh Festival* arrives at Stratford FLT from the nearby diesel depot in order to take out a 'Freightliner' service for Garston, on Merseyside.
Camera: Nikon FM2, film rating: 300ASA
Exposure: 10secs @ f4

Brian Morrison

Bristol Temple Meads in the 1980s

Gloucester RC&W Class 119 dmu No. L581, with DMC W51095 leading, waits for the appropriate time to depart from Temple Meads on 8th June 1982 forming the 23.15 train to Cardiff Central. In the opposite platform, a Cravens Class 105 dmu with leading DMC No. M50812 (later renumbered to 53812 in order to avoid confusion on the BR 'TOPS' computer with the Class 50s), pauses with the 21.50 service from Taunton to Swindon.
Camera: Bronica EC, film rating: 400ASA
Exposure: 30secs @ f5.6

Brian Morrison

On the same summer night in 1982, Class 31/1 No. 31257 arrives at Temple Meads station with an up parcels train.
Camera: Bronica EC, film rating: 400ASA
Exposure: 40secs @ f5.6

Brian Morrison

On the evening of 21st December 1980, "Hoover" No. 50038 *Formidable* is about to depart from Temple Meads with the 16.45 Sunday service from Plymouth to Paddington, and will be followed away from the station by Class 45/0 'Peak' No. 45013 hauling the Newcastle TPO. Techniques in night photography vary and a short exposure in this instance has resulted in a more natural 'night' appearance to the scene but, of course, some of the detail which would, otherwise have been seen in the shadowed areas has been lost.
Camera: Praktisix II, film rating: 400ASA
Exposure: 10secs @ f8

Geoff Gillham

Opposite top:
At Bristol Temple Meads station on the warm evening of 8th June 1982, Class 31/4 No. 31422 prepares to remove empty stock from an earlier arrival to the carriage sidings at Malago Vale.
Camera: Mamiya 645, film rating: 400ASA
Exposure: 20secs @ f5.6

Colin Marsden

Opposite below:
On 14th January 1983, Class 40 No. 40058 is ready to depart from Temple Meads station with the 12.10 Penzance-Glasgow parcels train. At this time the Class 40 "Whistlers", despite their rapidly diminishing numbers, were probably more common in Bristol than at any other time since the mid-1960s.
Camera: Mamiya 645, film rating: 200ASA
Exposure: 10secs @ f5.6

John Chalcraft

On 8th June 1982, Class 33/0 "Crompton" No. 33028 arrives at Bristol Temple Meads station on time with the 20.30 service from Portsmouth Harbour, a journey time of just over two and a half hours.
Camera: Bronica EC, film rating: 400ASA
Exposure: 5secs @ f4

Brian Morrison

Forming a High Speed Train (HST) service to Paddington on 30th November 1983. InterCity 125 set No. 253005 prepares to depart Temple Meads station on its journey through the night.
Camera: Mamiya 645, film rating: 400ASA
Exposure: 20secs @ f5.6

Colin Marsden

Three withdrawn Class 55 'Deltics' are lined up outside Doncaster Works on 26th February 1982 in preparation for the adulation of the hordes which were due to descend on the following day for a special 'Deltic Open Day'. Nos 55016 *Gordon Highlander*, 55011 *The Royal Northumberland Fusiliers* and 55008 *The Green Howards* are the locomotives involved. Both 55008 and 55016 have since been preserved but 55011 succumbed to the cutter's torch in November 1982.

Camera: Mamiya 645, film rating: 400ASA
Exposure: 30secs @ f11

Colin Marsden

After Hours at the 'Plant'

Specially posed outside Doncaster Works attached to merry-go-round (mgr) hoppers for publicity photographs to be taken, the first of the Class 58 fleet to be constructed at the 'Plant', No. 58001, makes an impressive sight under the night sky.

Camera: Hasselblad, film rating: 125ASA
Exposure: 1sec @ f8 under floodlights

British Rail

Nocturnal Freight

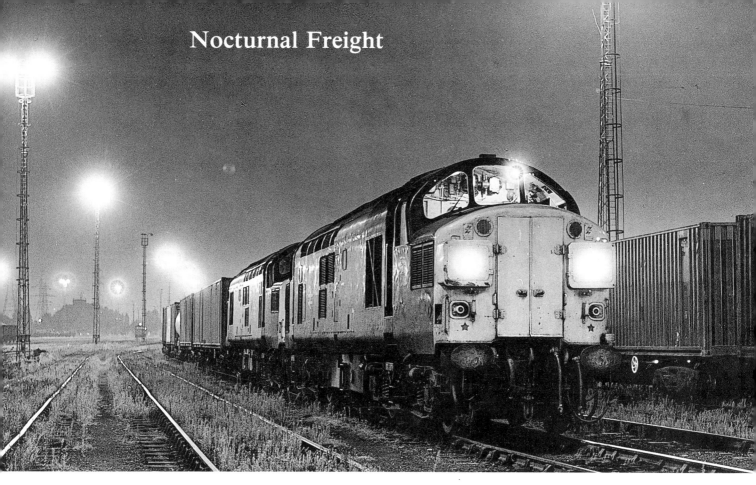

The 18.58 Tilbury-Glasgow Gushetfaulds 'Freightliner' prepares to head northwards from Temple Mills yards on 18th October 1985, powered by Class 37s Nos 37100 and 37113 working in multiple.
Camera: Nikon FM2, film rating: 300ASA
Exposure: 20secs @ f2.8

Brian Morrison

Normally, freight runs through Perth during the night hours without hindrance but on 21st September 1985, BRC&W Class 27/0 Bo-Bo, No. 27002 was halted for a short time by signals enabling this photograph to be taken of southbound empty coal wagons from Inverness.
Camera: Mamiya 645, film rating: 400ASA
Exposure: 20secs @ f5.6

Cyril Loftus

No sooner did BR Class 56 Co-Co No. 56095 grind to a halt in Derby station due to adverse signals, than the signalman realised his error and allowed the train of loaded mgr hoppers to proceed on its southward journey. With little time to spare, this photograph was obtained just before the load commenced to move again.
Camera: Nikon FM2, film rating: 400ASA
Exposure: 2secs @ f2

Brian Morrison

Bound for Stratford FLT in East London, Class 47/0 No. 47213 is brought to a stand on the York station centre line in the early hours of 8th February 1980 for a crew change. A fine drizzle is falling from the sky, enhancing the scene pictorially but forcing the photographer to stay under cover of the station canopy in order to protect his camera from unwelcome, and potentially damaging, rainwater.
Camera: Mamiya 645, film rating: 400ASA
Exposure: 30secs @ f8

Cyril Loftus

The station lighting at Doncaster is particularly conducive to night photography, providing not only good illumination but excellent contrast as can be seen here. On 10th September 1979, a southbound mgr coal train hauled by Class 47/0 No. 47212 is halted on the centre road through the station to allow the passenger service in the platform to depart first.
Camera: Mamiya 645, film rating: 400ASA
Exposure: 10secs @ f5.6

Colin Marsden

The 18.40 Kennett to Mountsorrel train of 'Redland' hoppers hauled by Class 20s Nos 20182 and 20017 is held in the loop outside Ely station on 17th January 1989 awaiting the passage of a Liverpool Street–King's Lynn 'Network Express'. Being a long way from the station lighting, a 300mm telephoto lens was used and, in consequence, the exposure was a long one. Happily the driver remained fairly still throughout.
Camera: Nikon FM2, film rating: 400ASA
Exposure: 3mins @ f6.3

Brian Morrison

A last look at the old UCV clay wagons. On 15th September 1982, Class 47/4 No. 47475 pauses at Exeter St Davids with a rake of condemned stock bound for Sharpness.
Camera: Mamiya 645, film rating: 400ASA
Exposure: 35secs @ f8

Colin Marsden

Class 73/1 electro-diesels, in contrasting liveries, stand on No. 49 road at Clapham Junction on 28th January 1986 heading the 20.28 Newhaven-Tolworth RMC aggregates train made up of the company's distinctive orange-coloured hoppers. The locomotives are Nos 73133 with wrap-around yellow front and large BR logo and No.73108 which is painted in InterCity colours for hauling "Gatwick Express" workings.
Camera: Nikon FM2, film rating: 400ASA
Exposure: 8secs @ f5.6

Colin Marsden

'Sleepers'

On the night of 8th February 1980, the 22.55 Newcastle–King's Cross 'Sleeper' was unexpectedly stopped for adverse signals in York station, enabling the photographer to quickly set up his tripod and catch this fine picture of 'Deltic' No. 55021 *Argyll and Sutherland Highlander*.
Camera: Mamiya 645, film rating: 400ASA
Exposure: 20secs @ f8   *Cyril Loftus*

Opposite top:
Class 47/4 No. 47476 waits for passengers at Penzance station on 12th September 1979, prior to departure with the 21.35 sleeping car service for Paddington.
Camera: Praktisix II, film rating: 400ASA
Exposure: 10secs @ f8
                          Geoff Gillham

Opposite below:
Class 47/4 No. 47570, which was allocated to London Stratford at the time, finds itself at Perth station on 23rd August 1984 in charge of the 22.42 'Sleeper' to Euston. The Mk 3 SLE (Sleeper Either Class) and SLEP (Sleeper Either Class with Pantry) coaches in evidence here were introduced from 1981/82 to replace the aging Mk 1 vehicles which had been in use, in some instances, since 1957.
Camera: Olympus OM1, film rating: 400ASA
Exposure: 30secs @ f5.6   *Michael J. Collins*

Hauling 'Sleeper' stock to form the 22.00 for King's Cross, Class 31/4 No. 31410 arrives at Leeds station from Neville Hill sidings on 21st May 1982.
Camera: Mamiya 645, film rating: 400ASA
Exposure: 20secs @ f8

                          Colin Marsden

During the period in 1988/89 that the GEC Class 91 locomotives were under evaluation, the stock which made up one of the test trains was formed of spare Mk 3 sleeping coaches from the King's Cross overnight services which, for operational reasons, had been transferred to Euston. Attached to this stock and ready for trials again on the following morning, No. 91001 rests outside Bounds Green depot on 30th August 1988.
Camera: Nikon FM2, film rating: 400ASA
Exposure: 20secs @ f5.6

Brian Morrison

On 20th May 1983, "Hoover" No. 50021 *Rodney* stands in Truro station with the 21.35 Penzance-Paddington 'Sleeper' shortly before the introduction of Mk 3 sleeping car stock.
Camera: Praktisix II, film rating: 400ASA
Exposure: 12secs @ f8

Geoff Gillham

The 22.30 service from Invernesss to Edinburgh and Glasgow Queen Street stations includes sleeping accommodation. On 21st September 1985, the train waits at Perth with Class 47/4 No. 47469 *Glasgow Chamber of Commerce* providing the motive power.
Camera: Mamiya 645, film rating: 400ASA
Exposure: 30secs @ f8

Cyril Loftus

Class 71s at Victoria

Prior to their final withdrawal from service in November 1977, the Southern Region's fleet of Class 71 electric locomotives was frequently utilised for overnight newspaper trains from London Victoria. Shortly before 03.00 on the morning of 17th September 1974, No. 71002 awaits departure time with a vans train for Maidstone. One wonders why just one light should be on at this hour in the office block building in the background?

Camera: Bronica S2a, film rating: 400ASA
Exposure: 30secs @ f5.6

Brian Morrison

Class 71 No. 71005 purrs to itself in the early hours of the same day, waiting to venture out into the darkness with the 03.00 newspaper train for Dover Western Docks.

Camera: Bronica S2a, film rating: 400ASA
Exposure: 1min @ f8

Brian Morrison

Granite City
After Dark

A pair of BRC&W Class 26/0s, Nos 26034 and 26041, are rostered for the 18.40 Aberdeen-Inverness service on 14th November 1984 and await the appointed time before heading away from the station confines of the Granite City.
Camera: Nikon FM2, film rating: 400ASA
Exposure: 8secs @ f4

Colin Marsden

In the same position as the scene above but photographed from the opposite platform on the previous day, Class 47 No. 47120 waits to leave Aberdeen station with the 17.40 to Inverness. This locomotive was named *RAF Kinloss* at Forres in June 1985 but had the plates removed on being re-allocated away from the Scottish Region.
Camera: Nikon FM2, film rating: 400ASA
Exposure: 10secs @ f4

Colin Marsden

A frost-encrusted Class 27/0 No. 27002 arrives at Aberdeen station on a bitterly cold February evening in 1983 in charge of the 17.40 train from Inverness. It is at times such as this that both cab and train heating are vital – and thermal underwear would also appear in order for the photographer!
Camera: Mamiya 645, film rating: 400ASA
Exposure: 45secs @ f8

Cyril Loftus

A dramatic study at the Granite City on the night of 13th October 1974, with Class 40 "Whistler" No. 40173 showing code 1E43 in the route indicator panel for the 20.15 departure for King's Cross.
Camera: Mamiya C3, film rating: 200ASA
Exposure: 20secs @ f8

Cyril Loftus

Night Pilots

Most major termini and inter-change stations have need for a locomotive to act as a station pilot for shunting vans, coaches and the like. Many of these movements take place at night, as witness this scene at Exeter St Davids station on 14th July 1983 with Class 08 No. 08954 shunting a van to attach to an up TPO. In the background, the yellow front of a Class 33 is illuminated by the yard lighting.
Camera: Mamiya 645, film rating: 400ASA
Exposure: 10secs @ f5.6

Colin Marsden

At Liverpool Street station on 10th January 1986, the night pilot is Class 08 No. 08541, which is shown here having brought in vans to make up a parcels train for loading.
Camera: Mamiya 645, film rating: 400ASA
Exposure: 15secs @ f8

Brian Beer

The crew of the station shunter at Derby on 23rd June 1983 have taken a short break from activities and allowed an opportunity for the photographer, with the assistance of a wide-angle lens, to capture on film this Class 08 No. 08623 pictured against a foreground of platform trolleys.
Camera: Nikon FE, film rating: 400ASA
Exposure: 45secs @ f8

Brian Morrison

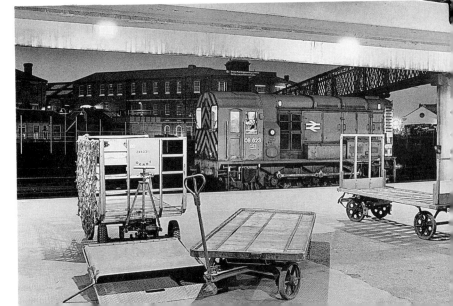

Sandwiching a variety of rolling stock which is made up of a fine example of an SR 'B' van, a standard BG, two CCT parcels vans and a PMV, two Class 08s, Nos 08877 and 08878, arrange a train at Sheffield on 28th January 1980. The apparatus in the foreground is a water filler for diesel locomotive steam heating boilers.
Camera: Mamiya 645, film rating: 400ASA
Exposure: 30secs @ f8

Colin Marsden

A Class 03 0-6-0 shunter No. 03079, now withdrawn, pauses on the centre road at Newcastle station between shunts on 20th May 1982, coupled to the usual ZSV shunting truck.
Camera: Mamiya 645, film rating: 400ASA
Exposure: 10secs @ f5.6

Colin Marsden

Introduced between 1952 and 1962, the mammoth fleet of 0-6-0 diesel shunters which now make up Class 08 once totalled 1,193 locomotives. That many are still in service to this day is testimony to their robustness and reliability for well over three decades. On 4th February 1983, No. 08500 shunts sleeping car stock at Leeds station.
Camera: Nikon FM2, film rating: 400ASA
Exposure: 10secs @ f4

Colin Marsden

Derby Nights

On the misty evening of 20th February 1985, Class 45/0 'Peak' No. 45070 has charge of a parcels train in platform 4 of Derby station. While loading takes place, the previously quiet station complex suddenly comes to life (below) with arrivals of a local service in the form of a BR Swindon Class 120 dmu and two InterCity 125 High Speed Trains forming the 15.11 Plymouth-York and 17.30 Newcastle-Bristol services. Soon all three trains will have proceeded on their way and the 'Peak' will once again become the station's sole occupant.

Camera: Nikon FM2, film rating: 400ASA
Exposures: 40secs @ f5.6 and 10secs @ f2.8 respectively
Both Brian Morrison

An evening Nottingham-Crewe Class 120 cross-country dmu service, with DMBC No. 53735 leading, makes the required reversal at Derby on 28th June 1983.
Camera: Nikon FM2, film rating: 400ASA
Exposure: 5secs @ f2.8

Brian Morrison

The two prototype 'Sprinter' Class 150 3-car dmus which were introduced in 1984 for evaluation trials were operating the Derby-Matlock services on the evening of 20th February 1985. (Left) set No. 150002 arrives at Derby with the 18.10 from Matlock and (below), No. 150001 forms the 19.10 return working. No. 150002 was modified at Derby in 1987 with new engines, a revised seating layout and the inclusion of partial air-conditioning, re-classified as 154 and given the running number of 154002 in order to prove equipment intended for the 'Super Sprinter' classes.
Cameras: Nikon FM2s, film rating: 400ASA
Exposures: 8secs @ f2.8

Colin Marsden & Brian Morrison

'Westerns' and a 'Warship'

Just five weeks before withdrawal from service, Class 52 'Western' No. D1048 *Western Lady* ticks over at the fuel siding at Westbury depot on 19th January 1977. In the distance, the somewhat ghostly presence is Class 08 shunter No. 08225.
Camera: Praktisix II, film rating: 400ASA
Exposure: 45secs @ f8

Geoff Gillham

During the final months of the Class 52's operations, several of the London commuter services utilised 'Western' motive power. On 18th December 1976, No. D1041 *Western Prince* stands at Paddington after arrival with an overnight service from West Wales.
Camera: Pentax KM 35mm, film rating: 125ASA
Exposure: 5secs @ f3.5

Colin Marsden

The "Western China Clay" enthusiasts' special was a RPPR classic railtour. Enthusiasm for the last days of the 'Westerns' was at its height and some 600 people travelled overnight from London to visit Cornish branch lines in freezing temperatures and, what is more, they enjoyed it! No. D1023 *Western Fusilier* stops at Plymouth on the outward run of 4th December 1976 while some of the passengers partake of refreshment in the station buffet where special arrangements had been made for it to stay open for the train, regardless of the hour, as no buffet facilities were available on board.
Camera: Pentax KM 35mm, film rating: 125ASA
Exposure: 45secs @ f6.3

Colin Marsden

As initial replacements for the Western Region steam locomotives, the 'Warship' class B-B fleet were not highly thought of by the railway enthusiasts of the early 1960s, but when one considers the mileage which the locomotives put up, the heavy loads which they regularly hauled and the limited knowledge of diesel hydraulic power at hand during maintenance, many are now of the opinion that the class was very much under-rated in their day. On 7th March 1964, Class 43 No. D838 *Rapid* stands at Crewe station at 02.00 with the Glasgow/Manchester-Penzance train which carried sleeping cars between Manchester and Plymouth.
Camera: Rollieflex, film rating: 200ASA
Exposure: approx. 30secs @ f8

John Clarke

The 22.10 overnight sleeping car train for Paddington stands at Penzance station on a balmy August night in 1975 headed by Class 52 C-C No. 1068 *Western Reliance*. Light falling on the train from the station lamps was minimal, thus requiring a fairly long time exposure in order to record this scene.
Camera: Bronica S2a, film rating: 400ASA
Exposure: 2mins @ F5.6

Brian Morrison

Night Parcels

The Rolls-Royce powered, BR Derby built Class 127 dmus were introduced for passenger services in 1959, a number being converted for carriage of parcels and newspaper traffic in 1985, following electrification of the "Bedpan" services from St Pancras to Bedford. At Euston station on 20th February 1988, a 2-car Class 127 unit No. 910, headed by car No. 55970, fronts another unit of the same type and four vans making up a parcels train for the North. The bird motif painted below the centre windscreen signifies that the vehicle is allocated to Manchester Longsight TMD.

Camera: Mamiya 645, film rating: 400 ASA
Exposure: 2secs @ f8

Brian Beer

One can almost feel the frost in the night air in this scene taken on 12th January 1979 in Woking down yard, with Class 73/1 electro-diesel No. 73115 preparing to move away under diesel power with a vans train for Clapham Junction. This locomotive had to be withdrawn from service in April 1982 following a serious accident at Croydon and was cut up at Selhurst depot in August of the same year.

Camera: Pentax KM 35mm, film rating: 125ASA
Exposure: 1min @ f8

Colin Marsden

Christmas parcels pack the platform at Exeter St Davids station on 18th December 1978 as Class 50 No. 50040 *Leviathan* makes the scheduled stop with the 16.30 Paddington-Plymouth service. In the opposite platform, Class 33/0 No. 33026 waits for departure time with the last train of the day for Salisbury.

Camera: Praktisix II, film rating: 400ASA
Exposure: 15secs @ f6.3

Geoff Gilham

On 3rd April 1982, Class 46 1Co-Co1 No. 46049 splutters away to itself in one of the down, through platforms at Newcastle station heading the 14.52 parcels train from Liverpool Lime Street to Edinburgh.
Camera: Mamiya 645, film rating: 400ASA
Exposure: 45secs @ f8

Cyril Loftus

In charge of a vans train for Gloucester, Class 37 No. 37210 stands at Cardiff Central station on 9th June 1982 while loading takes place. Lighting from the platform side of the train is quite good, but only reflected light and some street lamp illumination are in evidence from this standpoint, resulting in an exposure three times longer than is necessary with the conventional platform-side viewpoint.
Camera: Bronica EC, film rating: 400ASA
Exposure: 45secs @ f5.6

Brian Morrison

Although it is 06.00 on the morning of 3rd April 1982, there is yet no sign of the dawn at Glasgow Queen Street as Class 37 No. 37111 prepares to move parcels stock away from the station. This locomotive now carries number 37326 and *Glengarnock* nameplates.
Camera: Mamiya 645, film rating: 400ASA
Exposure: 30secs @ f8

Cyril Loftus

At an hour when most self respecting railway photographers are well and truly in the land of nod, a Class 73/1 No. 73107 is photographed at London Victoria station on 17th September 1977 ready to power the 03.27 vans train to Eastbourne.
Camera: Bronica S2a, film rating: 400ASA
Exposure: 30secs @ f8

Brian Morrison

On 11th September 1981, the 19.18 York to Ferme Park, Hornsey, parcels train was surprisingly provided with 'Deltic' haulage. Luckily, a photographer happened to be on hand at Doncaster and was able to record this scene of the Class 55 No. 55014 *The Duke of Wellington's Regiment* preparing to move off again towards London.

Camera: Mamiya 645, film rating: 400ASA
Exposure: 20secs @ f5.6

Colin Marsden

Colchester's St Botolph's station is rarely seen in print, but the appearance there on 15th March 1988 of a Class 308/2 emu parcels unit No. 308995 prompted a photographer's visit. In reality this was not a parcels service but a special charter for the evening by the local BR First Aid team in order that they could produce a realistic environment for a first aid competition which they held inside it.

Camera: Olympus OM1, film rating: 400ASA
Exposure: 30secs @ f6.3 + flash

Michael J. Collins

With just three passenger coaches but seven vans, obviously parcels are of prime importance on the 18.00 Penzance-Bristol Temple Meads service seen here on the scheduled stop at Teignmouth station on 17th September 1981. Motive power is provided by Class 50 No. 50003 *Temeraire*.

Camera: Praktisix II, film rating: 400ASA
Exposure: 10secs @ f5.6

Geoff Gilham

69

Evening Off-Peak – Provincial Sector

The fleet of BR Swindon built Class 123 InterCity dmus was originally used on outer suburban services from Paddington, being transferred to the Eastern Region during the mid-1970s, where they held sway on the Manchester-Hull trains for a number of years, until final withdrawal from service in August 1984. On 8th September 1981, a Class 123 unit led by Driving Motor Second (DMS) No. 52100 forms the 19.45 service from Manchester Piccadilly to Hull and is seen here making the scheduled stop at Doncaster.
Camera: Mamiya 645, film rating: 400ASA
Exposure: 10secs @ f5.6

Colin Marsden

The old and new orders at Doncaster on 7th November 1984. Clearly showing the differences in design concept which have taken place over the quarter century since their respective introduction, a Metro-Cammell Class 101 dmu and a Leyland National/BREL Derby Class 141 Railbus almost invite comparison as they stand in adjacent platforms with trains to Hull and Leeds.
Camera: Nikon FM2, film rating: 400ASA
Exposure: 15secs @ f5.6

Colin Marsden

Whilst the suburban units of British Rail were intended for operating with heavy loading on short, start and stop, rush hour commuter services, their importance to general travel throughout most of the day and night, in and around the large cities cannot be underestimated. On 4th February 1983, a Class 101 dmu led by Driving Trailer Composite (DTC) No. E56218 (now 54218) and BRC&W Class 110 with DMBC No. E51817 at the driving end, form respective services for Harrogate and Bradford due to depart from Leeds, at 22.50 and 22.05 respectively.
Camera: Bronica EC, film rating: 800ASA
Exposure: 10secs @ f5.6

Brian Morrison

The 16.33 Peterborough to Norwich train makes the scheduled Ely stop on 17th January 1989 formed of Metro-Cammell Class 156 'Sprinter' No. 156417. Introduced in 1987, the first batch of 29 of these dmus is based at Norwich Crown Point T&RSMD for working the Provincial Sector's Midland cross-country services.
Camera: Nikon FM2, film rating: 400ASA
Exposure: 5secs @ f2.8

Brian Morrison

On 9th February 1983, the 21.20 Preston-Windermere train makes the scheduled Lancaster stop on time at 21.45 formed of a BR Swindon Class 120 Cross-Country dmu which consists of DMBC No. M51581, Trailer Second (TS) No. M59587 and DMS No. M51585. The two Driving Motor vehicles were later converted for Parcels Sector use and respectively renumbered 55937 and 55940. Both were subsequently withdrawn from service in March 1987, outliving the TS, which was withdrawn in May 1986, by some ten months.
Camera: Bronica EC, film rating: 400ASA
Exposure: 5secs @ f4

Brian Morrison

Not only is the station at Doncaster well lit, but the approaches too have an abundance of illumination. Standing in the stabling point just beneath the well known multi-storey car park which overlooks the station, BR Derby Class 114 dmu with DTS No. E56041 (later 54041) carrying the Cleethorpes destination blind, awaits the next call of duty on 10th September 1981.
Camera: Mamiya 645, film rating: 400ASA
Exposure: 20secs @ f6.3

Colin Marsden

With a new moon in the sky over Buxton station in February 1985, two BRC&W Class 104 dmus stand at each of the only two station platforms which remain in use. With the indicator blind showing 'Piccadilly', DMS No. M53421 actually leads the 18.08 for Manchester Oxford Road; the route indicator panel on DMS No. M53459 correctly shows 'Manchester', this train forming the 19.08 departure for the same destination.
Camera: Nikon FM2, film rating: 400ASA
Exposure: 4secs @ f2.8

Brian Morrison

An excellent study of the north bays at Newcastle station on 20th May 1982, with nothing to be seen but the ubiquitous Class 101 Metro-Cammell dmus forming a variety of local night services.
Camera: Mamiya 645, film rating: 400ASA
Exposure: 15secs @ f5.6

Colin Marsden

On 24th January 1981, BR Derby Class 108 twin, made up of DMBS No. M50967 (now 53967) and DTC No. M56250 (now 54250), forms a dmu service for Whitehaven and awaits departure time in the bay platform at Carlisle. A longer than normal film exposure was needed in this instance in order to use a camera lens aperture small enough to retain both the unit and platform 'brutes' in sharp focus.
Camera: Bronica EC, film rating: 400ASA
Exposure: 40secs @ f11

Brian Morrison

Class 304 emu No. 304019 collects passengers at Rugby on 2nd March 1984 prior to departure as the 19.10 to Stafford. Although the exposure time was as short as practical, there is still discernible movement from at least one of the folk on the platform.
Camera: Nikon FM2. Film rating: 400ASA
Exposure: 2secs @ f2.8

Brian Morrison

– And Network SouthEast

Above:
Hauling two sets of Class 438 4TC stock, Class 33/0 No. 33049 waits to leave Watford Junction station with a return 'Footex' special to Maidstone East following the Watford v Maidstone F.A. cup tie. This was the second of two similar trains for Maidstone supporters, the first having departed shortly before, behind another "Crompton", No. 33023.
Camera: Mamiya 645, film rating: 400ASA
Exposure: 15secs @ f6.3

Brian Beer

Opposite top:
With the Network SouthEast Sector digital clocks showing precisely 21.35 and 28secs, the 21.45 service for Bournemouth and Poole awaits custom at Waterloo on 10th November 1988 formed of Class 442 "Wessex Electric" emu No. 2417.
Camera: Nikon FM2, film rating: 400ASA
Exposure: 1sec @ f2.8

Brian Morrison

Opposite below:
The 17.53 Portsmouth Harbour service is ready to commence its journey from Reading on 17th November 1984, formed of Class 204 Eastleigh-built demu No. 1401 which appears to be in ex-works' condition. The four units which made up this class were formed in 1979 when the Driving Trailers from withdrawn Class 206 "Tadpole" units were inserted as ordinary trailers into the remaining 2-car units of Class 205, this example having previously been numbered 1108.
Camera: Olympus OM1, film rating: 400ASA
Exposure: 30secs @ f8

Michael J. Collins

The Southern Region's purpose-built Class 455 replacement stock for a large proportion of their suburban network, commenced delivery from BREL York Works in late 1982. The Class 508 emu fleet was then transferred to the Liverpool area to displace the 'Merseyrail' emus which, in a number of cases, dated from 1938. With both cab and station lights shining brightly, the driver of the 17.52 emu for Waterloo awaits the guard's bell at Guildford on 3rd November 1984 before starting unit No. (45)5839 on its 30 mile journey.
Camera: Nikon FM2, film rating: 400ASA
Exposure: 10secs @ F4.5

Colin Marsden

During the very severe winter of 1986/87, the Southern Region encountered considerable difficulty in obtaining power from its third rail following heavy snowfalls, and in many instances, was forced to use diesel locomotives to haul electric stock in·order to maintain at least some services. Kent was the worst hit of all the counties with a number of towns and villages cut off from all types of transport for several days. On 17th January 1987, Class 56 No. 56062 (since named *Mountsorrell*) pauses briefly at Rochester while working a Victoria-Ramsgate service which is made up of 2EPB and 4EPB emu stock.
Camera: Mamiya 645, film rating: 400ASA
Exposure: 10secs @ f8   *Brian Beer*

A BREL York constructed Class 319 emu No. 319024 waits to depart from St Pancras on 17th February 1989, forming the 18.01 Network SouthEast commuter service for Bedford. On the centre road, Class 08 shunter No. 08612 prepares to move Travelling Post Office vans into a platform road in order to accommodate both postal arrivals and Post Office staff.
Camera: Nikon FM2, film rating: 400ASA
Exposure: 2secs @ f4.5
                                                         Brian Morrison

The suburban platforms at King's Cross are under the control of Network SouthEast, who, in 1988, dug out and reopened the closed platform 11 in order to improve rush hour services. It also provides a position within the station for 'stabling' purposes, without the necessity of a unit having to travel as ecs back to Hornsey depot. On 10th November 1988, Class 317 units Nos 317342 and 317367 occupy platforms 10 and 11 respectively, with the train on the left forming the 20.35 to Peterborough and the further unit being out of service. The platform was swarming with travellers at the time of the photograph and to eliminate them appearing on film as a blurr, a long exposure was used with a small lens aperture.
Camera: Nikon FM2, film rating: 400ASA
Exposure: 45secs @ f16

Brian Morrison

In platform 9 at Moorgate station on 8th February 1988, Class 313 emu No. 313024 forms the 18.34 local service for Hertford North. With the platform lighting being particularly bright, heavy shadows result around the wall on the other side of the train and also around the unit bogies. A flash 'fill-in' has solved the problem.
Camera: Nikon FM2, film rating: 400ASA
Exposure 1/30th sec @ f5.6 plus electronic flash

Brian Morrison

Newspaper Traffic

With the icicles hanging from the bodysides of Class 45/0 'Peak' No. 45058 testifying to the extreme cold prevailing, an evening newspaper train awaits departure from St Pancras on 9th February 1985.
Camera: Mamiya 645, film rating: 400ASA
Exposure: 30secs @ f11

Brian Beer

Loading Sunday newspapers for the last time at Paddington in July 1988. Following problems within the newspaper industry, resulting from a move away from the traditional offices in Fleet Street, coupled with the introduction of new technology, the distribution of national newspapers was transferred to the roads.
Camera: Mamiya 645, film rating: 400ASA
Exposure: 1/60th sec @ f8 plus electronic flash

Brian Beer

A dedicated newspaper packing van at Paddington in July 1988. All different newspapers from the various printing groups were lumped together in vehicles of this type, where 'on the move' packing and distribution was undertaken by special packing staff. Today only a few magazines are still transported by rail in this manner.
Camera: Mamiya 645, film rating: 400ASA
Exposure: 10secs @ f11

Brian Beer

Painted in the distinctive livery of the Network SouthEast Sector, Class 47/4 No. 47582 *County of Norfolk* awaits departure from Paddington on 16th January 1988 with the 00.50 newspaper train for Bristol Temple Meads. The considerable volume of newspapers transported overnight by British Rail was a major source of revenue and transference of the business to the roads is to be regretted on more than one count.
Camera: Mamiya C3, film rating: 400ASA
Exposure: 10secs @ f5.6

Brian Beer

In the early hours of 7th October 1974, a Class 74 electro-diesel locomotive No. 74009 faces the night with the 02.15 'Newspapers' to Bournemouth.
Camera: Bronica S2a, film rating: 200ASA
Exposure: 30secs @ f8

Brian Morrison

Class 45/1 'Peak' No. 45104 *The Royal Warwickshire Fusiliers* awaits departure from St Pancras station with a newspaper train on the misty evening of 16th January 1988.
Camera: Mamiya 645, film rating: 400ASA
Exposure: 20secs @ f11

Brian Beer

Beneath the seemingly cavernous roof arches of Brunel's Paddington station on 23rd January 1988, Class 50 No. 50042 *Triumph* awaits the time for departure with train 1C03, the 23.15 'Newspapers' for Penzance.
Camera: Mamiya 645, film rating: 400ASA
Exposure: 30secs @ f5.6

Brian Beer

Whistling in the Dark

A fine night portrait of Class 40 No. 40010 at Crewe station on 12th September 1979. This locomotive once carried the name *Empress of Britain*.
Camera: Pentax 6x7, film rating: 400ASA
Exposure: 45secs @ f11

John Vaughan

Opposite:
On 25th February 1981, Class 40 "Whistler" No. 40099 undergoes maintenance at Reddish depot. Note the missing buffer.
Camera: Pentax 6x7, film rating: 400ASA
Exposure: 20secs @ f8

John Vaughan

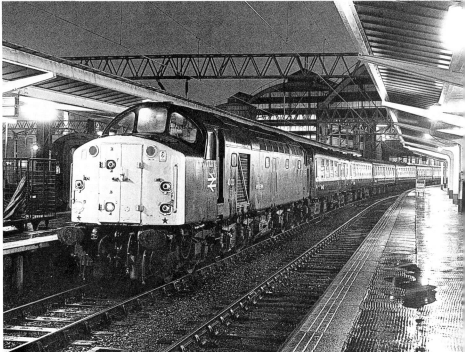

Similarly-named Class 40 No. 40033 *Empress of England* stands in Manchester Piccadilly station on 10th February 1984 with empty coaching stock for Longsight depot. The official nameplate for this locomotive had been removed some time ago and the one on display here is merely painted on.
Camera: Olympus OM1, film rating: 125ASA
Exposure: 15secs @ f8

Kim Fullbrook

At 05.50 on the morning of 8th November 1981, "Whistler" No. 40049 waits for the green signal at Doncaster station with a southbound vans train.
Camera: Mamiya 645, film rating: 400ASA
Exposure: 15secs @ f8

Gary Grafton

A.C. Electrics

City of Lancaster in the City of Lancaster! Hauling the 18.06 Edinburgh/18.23 Glasgow Central-Manchester Piccadilly service, Class 86/2 No. 86205, named after the city, makes the prescribed stop at Lancaster station on the night of 9th February 1983.
Camera: Bronica EC, film rating: 400ASA
Exposure: 20secs @ f5.6

Brian Morrison

The 10.35 Stranraer Harbour-Euston service glides to a stop at Rugby on 2nd March 1984 hauled by Class 87/0 No. 87005 *City of London*. The train has taken 7hr 20min to get this far and is timed to arrive in London in another 1¼ hours.
Camera: Nikon FM2, film rating: 400ASA
Exposure: 12secs @ f2.8

Brian Morrison

Class 86/2 No. 86209 *City of Coventry* comes to a stand beyond the platform end at Nuneaton on 1st March 1984 with the 18.05 Euston-Blackpool North train. Without normal platform lighting at this point, a flash gun was used for illumination while the camera lens was left open on a tripod.
Camera: Nikon FM2, film rating: 400ASA
Exposure: 2mins @ f2.8 + flash

Colin Marsden

In recent years, Carlisle has been a focal point for steam enthusiasts travelling on, or following, the various "Cumbrian Mountain" specials which traverse the Settle & Carlisle route. On 24th January 1981, ex-Southern Railway 4-6-0 *Lord Nelson* had arrived on a northbound working and Class 85 No. 85019 has backed onto the special for the return journey to Crewe and the south.
Camera: Bronica EC, film rating: 400ASA
Exposure: 30secs @ f8

Brian Morrison

On 4th October 1981, train 1V18, the 18.24 Sunday service from Manchester Piccadilly to Paddington stands in Birmingham New Street station behind the locomotive which had brought it thus far, Class 82 No. 82006. This locomotive will come off at this point to be exchanged for a diesel for the remainder of the journey.
Camera: Pentax 6x7, film rating: 400ASA
Exposure: 20secs @ f8

Norman E. Preedy

Third generation ac electric locomotive No. 90006 arrives at Wembley InterCity depot on the evening of 8th November 1988, having completed a successful evaluation test run to Glasgow and back with the first custom-built Driving Van Trailer (DVT), No. 82101 attached to the other end of the train.
Camera: Nikon FM2, film rating: 400ASA
Exposure: 5secs @ f5.6

Brian Morrison

Opposite top:
Working in multiple, Class 31/1s Nos 31222 and 31279 are here rostered for the 22.00 train for King's Cross and await commencement of the journey at Leeds station on 21st May 1982. A 2-car Class 108 dmu stands in the opposite platform with a local arrival from York.
Camera: Mamiya 645, film rating: 400ASA
Exposure: 15secs @ f5.6

Colin Marsden

Opposite below:
Class 33/1 'push-pull' fitted "Crompton" No. 33109 leads Class 33/0 No. 33019, of the standard variety, on the erstwhile centre road at Exeter St Davids for a 'banker' to assist with the climb to Exeter Central with a train of Meldon ballast on 1st September 1981.
Camera: Praktisix II, film rating: 400ASA
Exposure: 10secs @ f8

Geoff Gillham

Looking very similar indeed to the Class 90 locomotive illustrated above, DVT No. 82101 brings up the rear of the same test train which consists of Test Car *Prometheus* and two vehicles of BREL Derby's 'International' coach set.
Camera: Nikon FM2, film rating: 400ASA
Exposure: 5secs @ f5.6

Brian Morrison

Two's Company

Deltics

Class 55 'Deltic' No. 55009 *Alycidon* stands inside the well known King's Cross train shed on 22nd April 1981, ready to haul the 05.50 train to Aberdeen. The locomotive has been given the Finsbury Park depot 'treatment' and sports a distinctive white-painted cab.
Camera: Mamiya 645, film rating: 400ASA
Exposure 10secs @ f8

Colin Marsden

Powering the northbound "Aberdonian" express from King's Cross to Aberdeen on 29th October 1977, 'Deltic' No. 55006 *The Fife & Forfar Yeomanry* draws to a halt under the magnificent curving roof of York station.
Camera: Bronica S2a, film rating: 400ASA
Exposure: 1/4sec @ f2.8

Brian Morrison

A remarkable photograph of 'Deltic' No. 55013 *The Black Watch* 'letting off steam' at Doncaster station on 26th October 1981, whilst hauling the 00.05 King's Cross-Newcastle overnight train.
Camera: Mamiya 645, film rating: 400ASA
Exposure: 5secs @ f5.6

Gary Grafton

With the single exhaust providing the clue to this being merely an ecs working on one engine, No. 55018 *Ballymoss* waits at King's Cross on 18th November 1979 prior to moving away into Gasworks Tunnel.
Camera: Mamiya C3, film rating: 400ASA
Exposure: 30secs @ f8

Cyril Loftus

North of the Border

With the platform clock showing 16 minutes to go before departure is due, the 22.20 Sunday service to Dundee awaits custom at Edinburgh on 28th May 1988, formed of a BREL York-built Class 150/2 'Sprinter' No. 150257.
Camera: Nikon FM2, film rating: 400ASA
Exposure: 8secs @ f5.6

Brian Morrison

To drive the accelerated Edinburgh-Glasgow 'push-pull' expresses from the end of the train, remote from the Class 47/7 locomotive that provides the power, a fleet of 15 Mk2f Brake Second Open stock (BSOs) had their luggage vans converted to driving compartments, and were fitted with headlights, marker lights and tail lights below the newly provided front windows. No. 9707 of the fleet which was introduced in 1979/80, waits at Glasgow Queen Street station on 15th November 1984 for the time to depart with the 17.00 to Edinburgh.
Camera: Nikon FM2, film rating: 400ASA
Exposure: 25secs @ f8

Colin Marsden

Barclay Class 06 0-4-0 shunter No. 06002, with a short train of tanks at Dundee station on 12th February 1981, waits for the Class 101 dmu forming a local working, to depart from the opposite platform before 'receiving the road' to proceed.
Camera: Mamiya 645, film rating: 400ASA
Exposure: 30secs @ f8

Brian Beer

Two locomotives stabled overnight in Perth station are BRC&W Class 26/0 No. 26025 and Class 47/7 No. 47706 *Strathclyde* in 'Scotrail' livery.
Camera: Mamiya 645, film rating: 400ASA
Exposure: 30secs @ f8

Cyril Loftus

It is quite evident from these photographs that the lighting inside Glasgow Queen Street station is ideal for after dark photography. On the left, there is ample illumination falling upon BRC&W Class 27/0 No. 27048 heading empty stock to Cowlairs sidings off the 13.00 arrival from Oban, and below, Class 37 No. 37090 appears similarly bathed in light at the working end of the 16.50 train to Fort William.
Camera: Nikon FM2, film rating: 400ASA
Exposures: both 25secs @ f8

Both Colin Marsden

As one may imagine, photographs of the Millerhill to Inverness night goods train are not over abundant! An opportunity to record the working on film came about, however, on 21st September 1985 when a crew change took place at Perth. Motive power provided for the duty was Class 37 No. 37183.
Camera: Mamiya 645, film rating: 400ASA
Exposure: 30secs @ f8

Cyril Loftus

Booked for a High Speed Train but, in fact, operated on this occasion by a locomotive and stock, the 20.30 service from Aberdeen arrives at Edinburgh on 29th May 1988 only a few minutes late behind Class 47/4 No. 47595 *Confederation of British Industry.*
Camera: Nikon FM2, film rating: 400ASA
Exposure: 10secs @ f5.6

Brian Morrison

Action in a Flash

As mentioned earlier in this album, it is imperative that flash photography is not employed on a moving train without the express permission and the prior knowledge, and agreement of the crew. In this case everything was undertaken properly, as can be witnessed by the expectant expressions in the cab of 'Deltic' No. 55022 *Royal Scots Grey,* which is passing the site of Finsbury Park No. 6 signal box on the 2nd January 1982 with the "Deltic Scotsman Farewell" special.
Camera: Mamiya 645, film rating: 400ASA
Exposure: synchronised electronic flash @ f2.8

Brian Beer

On 21st November 1983, Class 50 No. 50050 *Fearless* enters Axminster station hauling the 16.18 Exeter St Davids-Waterloo service. Again the sudden flash was no surprise to the crew as prior arrangements for the photograph had been made during the previous stop at Honiton.
Camera: Nikon FM2, film rating: 400ASA
Exposure: electronic flash synchronised @ 1/250th sec @ f2

John Vaughan

Class 73/1 electro-diesel No. 73101 *Brighton Evening Argus* approaches Goring-by-Sea station's up starter signal on 16th November 1983, working a "Venice Simplon Orient Express" (VSOE) Pullman special, the 17.26 from Brighton to London Victoria via Barnham. The VSOE still runs but, alas, Goring's old semaphore signal is no more.
Camera: Nikon FM2, film rating: 400ASA
Exposure: electronic flash synchronised @ 1/125th sec @ F2.8

John Vaughan

There is almost a posed look about this photograph taken on 15th January 1977 but, in fact, the train was coming out of the tunnel into Moorgate station terminus at a good 20mph. The driver was expecting the flash and, as such, any possible hazard was avoided. The train is the 11.56 from Welwyn Garden City formed of Class 313 emu No. 313038.
Camera: Bronica EC, film rating: 400ASA
Exposure: electronic flash @ f5.6

Brian Morrison

The Southern Region's electric third-rail network is particularly vulnerable to the effects of ice and snow which can interrupt current collection. Taken during a blizzard at Goring-by-Sea on 8th December 1967, the electronic flash fitted to the camera has coincided with a flash from the 4CEP emu conductor rail shoe and produced this remarkable result.

Camera: Rollieflex, film rating: 400ASA
Exposure: electronic flash @ f5.6

John Vaughan

The second week of January 1987 produced some of the heaviest snowfalls and the coldest temperatures recorded in Great Britain for over 40 years. In addition to frozen points, trains frozen to the track or overhead lines and ice on conductor rails, strong winds caused considerable drifting which blocked a number of lines in the South East and resulted in the unprecedented sight of the Inverness-based snow blower working in Kent. On 18th January 1987, the Beilhack Self Propelled Rotary Snow Blower No. ADB968500 blasts a path along the freight only branch from Hoo Junction to the Isle of Grain at High Halstow, the first occasion that the machine had worked south of Perth.

Camera: Canon EF, film rating: 400ASA
Exposure: electronic flash @ f2.8

Ken Brunt

Preston Vespers

With power from the overhead catenary switched off for weekend maintenance, Brush Class 47/0 diesel electric No. 47191 provides haulage for 'dead' AEI/Metrovick Class 82 electric locomotive No. 82007 at Preston on 25th May 1980. The train in tow is the 21.15 Inverness-Kensington Olympia 'Motorail' service. Only reflected light is falling on the two locomotives, requiring a longer than normal exposure and resulting in this rather unusual effect to their bodysides.
Camera: Mamiya C3, film rating: 400ASA
Exposure: 45secs @ f5.6

Cyril Loftus

In the days when Class 87/0 No. 87026 carried the fine name of *Redgauntlet,* a Euston-Glasgow Central InterCity express makes the scheduled Preston stop on 7th March 1979. Although not the fault of the gentleman whose name is now perpetuated on the bodysides of this locomotive, its current name of *Sir Richard Arkright* does not have quite the same romance about it!
Camera: Pentax 6x7, film rating: 400ASA
Exposure: 30secs @ f6.3

John Vaughan

Just one year prior to withdrawal, Class 40 "Whistler" No. 40099 heads a northbound excursion special at Preston on 22nd October 1983. Observe the 'LMS Preston Station' sign which still survives from the days of pre-Nationalisation.
Camera: Mamiya 645, film rating: 400ASA
Exposure: 20secs @ f5.6

Brian Beer

Departmental

Class 47/0 No. 47116, one of five locomotives of the class that were once fitted with V12 engines and known as Class 48, stands at Exeter St Davids station on the night of 14th July 1983, hauling a departmental stone train from Meldon Quarry to Salisbury. The silver-painted roof panel identifies this as a Stratford, East London, allocated locomotive.
Camera: Pentax 6x7, film rating: 400ASA
Exposure: 20secs @ f8

Colin Marsden

High Speed Track Recording Coach No. DB999550 is seen here attached to the rear of the 19.05 Liverpool Lime Street-York train at Leeds on 21st May 1982. Although the vehicle contains a considerable amount of sophisticated equipment, including an on-board computer, and is required to operate annually over the majority of BR's main lines, it was merely in transit on this occasion.
Camera: Mamiya 645, film rating: 400ASA
Exposure: 10secs @ f5.6

Colin Marsden

One of the most common types of track maintenance machine to be seen on BR metals is the Plasser & Theurer 'tamper' which is capable of levelling, lining and tamping on just one passing of a line. The machines weigh 42 tons and are self-powered by a 165kW engine. On 8th September 1983, No. 73305 waits at Exeter St Davids station for the HST on the left to depart, when it will take up overnight occupation of the line.
Camera: Pentax 6x7, film rating: 400ASA
Exposure: 15secs @ f5.6

Colin Marsden

With a cold mist beginning to gather in the High Peak District, BR purpose-built snowplough No. ADM965228 and a Class 104 dmu trailer car No. M59228 stand at the Buxton station buffer-stops on 21st February 1985. Between the two can be glimpsed a Class 104 3-car dmu forming the 16.38 from Manchester Piccadilly which has arrived at 17.35, in accordance with the timetable.
Camera: Nikon FM2, film rating: 400ASA
Exposure: 10secs @ f2.8

Brian Morrison

The Southern Region's Waterloo & City Line, or the 'Drain' as it is known to most of the 13,000-odd commuters who use the service morning and evening between Waterloo and Bank stations, dates from 1898 and is operated by Class 487 sliding door stock emus which date from 1940 – the same year that Track Circuit Block was installed with two-aspect colour light signalling. A small depot for the underground units is situated at the Waterloo end of the 1½ mile line and this is the view of it which can be seen from the end of the platform, albeit with the advantage of a telephoto lens.
Camera: Bronica S2a, film rating: 400ASA
Exposure: 8secs @ f5.6

Brian Morrison

At Bank station on 11th May 1987, the sliding doors wait to be closed before the Class 487 emu can move away into the tunnel for Waterloo. Resulting from a sponsorship by Allied-Lyons, whose logo can be seen on the left of the door, this stock is today painted in the red, white, blue and grey livery of the Network SouthEast Sector. Available light in the 'Drain' is excellent and the photographer with a steady hand can even get away with a hand-held exposure such as this.
Camera: Nikon FM2, film rating: 400ASA
Exposure: 1/15sec @ f2

Brian Morrison

The route length of the Tyne & Wear Metro system is 35 miles, of which 27 miles are converted BR suburban routes, with approximately half of the eight miles of new construction being underground. At the terminus of St James on 18th April 1983, two of the 90 2-car units, constructed by Metro-Cammell for the system, stand with open doors awaiting custom for a North Shields service.
Camera: Canon AE1, film rating: 400ASA
Exposure: 1/60th sec @ f1.4

John Glover

A London Transport Jubilee Line train for Stanmore, consisting of 1972 Mk2 stock, awaits departure time at Charing Cross station on 13th May 1988. As with the Tyne & Wear Metro and Waterloo & City line scenes opposite, the lighting at any time of the day or night on the underground sections of the London Regional Transport system requires night photography technique although, for the most part, illumination is very good and a tripod and time exposure can often be dispensed with.
Camera: Nikon FM2, film rating: 400ASA
Exposure: 1/30th sec @ f2.8

Brian Morrison

At Euston station, on the London Transport Victoria Line, a Walthamstow train leaves the platform on 14th May 1984 consisting of Metro-Cammell 1967 stock. Station lighting here is excellent and with a large enough camera lens it is just possible to photograph a train on the move.
Camera: Nikon FM2, film rating: 400ASA
Exposure: 1/125th sec @ f1.4

Brian Morrison

Two Glasgow Underground trains pass at Ibrox on 22nd August 1980 formed of Metro-Cammell "Clockwork Orange" stock, a nickname quickly given to the new trains for the system which arrived in 1980 in the attractive livery of the Strathclyde Transport Executive. The system is a circular one of 6½ miles in length with a 4ft track gauge and tunnels of 11ft in diameter, compared with the 12ft of London Transport. Lighting is particularly conducive to photography and, once again, a tripod is not essential for results such as this to be obtained.
Camera: Canon AE1, film rating: 400ASA
Exposure: 1/125th sec @ f1.4

John Glover

Inclement Weather

With the temperature at Worcester on the evening of 11th February 1985 around the $-8°C$ mark, it took a hardy soul to record this snow-swept scene of Class 50 No. 50034 *Furious*, well behind time with the 17.05 service from Paddington to Hereford.
**Camera: Canon AE1, film rating: 400ASA
Exposure: 30secs @ f8**

Michael Rhodes

A snow-covered Waterloo station on Sunday, 9th December 1981, with the somewhat sparse services not being able to run to timetable. With Class 415, 423 and 508 emus in the platforms, two Class 73/1 electro-diesels, Nos 73114 and 73118, stand in the dock lines ready to provide emergency services on diesel power if required.
**Camera: Bronica EC, film rating: 400ASA
Exposure: 30secs @ f5.6**

Brian Morrison

On the same bitterly cold evening at Waterloo, Class 50 No. 50014 *Warspite* is coupled up and ready to move away with what should have been the 19.10 service for Exeter St Davids. Unfortunately the time was already 19.45 when this photograph was taken!

Camera: Bronica EC, film rating: 400ASA
Exposure: 30secs @ f5.6

Brian Morrison

Opposite top:

Although the purpose of the brazier on Carlisle station is to prevent the water standpipe and hose from freezing up, it is, nevertheless, a most welcome sight for the night photographer who is out on a winter quest. On 11th February 1983, a Class 101 Metro Cammell-dmu stands in platform 5.
Camera: Pentax 35mm, film rating: 400ASA Exposure: 20secs @ f8

Chris Davis

Opposite below:

On 12th February 1981, an intrepid night photographer braves the sub-zero temperatures which are prevalent at this time of the year in Scotland, and records Class 27 No. 27032 in Perth station performing steam-heating duty. The well-stocked brazier is to prevent the water supply pipe from freezing up.
Camera: Mamiya 645, film rating: 400ASA Exposure: 10secs @ f5.6

Brian Beer

Night People

Top right:

On late turn, the driver of the 22.15 Sunday local service to Dunblane on 29th May 1988, awaits any last minute custom for the train at Edinburgh, before moving his charge out of platform 15 and into the night. The service is formed of a 1960 BR Derby-built Class 108 dmu set No. 384 with DMBS No. 51936 leading.
Camera: Nikon FM2, film rating: 400ASA Exposure: 2secs @ f2.8

Brian Morrison

Centre right:

Heath Junction signal box, near Cardiff, was closed in November 1984, shortly after this photograph was taken. As can be observed, lighting at the time was still provided by gas lamps.
Camera: Canon AE1, film rating: 400ASA Exposure: 25secs @ f16

Michael Rhodes

Right:

The Traveller's Fare 'Quicksnack' kiosk on Derby station remains open through the night of 20th February 1985 and enjoys a lone customer.
Camera: Nikon FM2, film rating: 400ASA Exposure: synchronised electronic flash @ 1/200th sec @ f2.8

Brian Morrison

Class 415/1 4EPB emu No. 5184 stands at
Gravesend, Kent, on 10th November 1984 forming
the 18.58 stopping service to Charing Cross via
Sidcup and Lewisham.
Camera: Olympus OM1, film rating: 400ASA
Exposure: 30secs @ f5.6 + flash
Michael J. Collins

Making their way from the Railway Technical
Centre at Derby to the IVA'88 International Traffic
& Transport Exhibition in Hamburg, via Dover
Western Docks and Dunkerque, British Rail's
exhibits are hauled to Dover by Class 47/4
No. 47561, which stops at Hither Green, in South
East London, in the early hours of 21st May 1988 for
a crew change. In tow are Classes 89, 90 and 91
locomotives Nos 89001, 90008 and 91003 together
with Class 150/2 'Sprinter' No. 150263, 'Inter-
national' coaches RUM99523 and BFK99520 and
two match vehicles.
Camera: Nikon FM2, film rating: 400ASA
Exposure: 5secs @ f5.6 + flash
Brian Morrison

Most stations appear far more attractive at night and Worthing Central is no exception, the ornate bicycle shed showing up to particular advantage! On 12th November 1983, the 21.02 Brighton-Portsmouth Harbour 'Coastway' service is unusually worked by a Class 73/1 electro-diesel No. 73139.
Camera: Nikon FM2, film rating: 400ASA
Exposure: 15secs @ f4

John Vaughan

The long-haul Waterloo-Exeter trains come under the considerable umbrella of the Network SouthEast Sector and the locomotives that work the services are allocated to and serviced at Plymouth Laira depot, a long distance from the Sector boundaries. Making the scheduled stop at Sherborne on 27th November 1986, "Hoover" No. 50015 *Valiant* is the motive power provided for the 17.10 departure from the London terminus to Exeter St Davids.
Camera: Mamiya 645, film rating: 400ASA
Exposure: 30secs @ f4.5

Brian Beer

Signals & Signal Boxes

Dawn at Northolt Junction, in West London, on 3rd February 1985 – and nothing stirs except the pigeon.
Camera: Pentax 6x7, film rating: 400ASA
Exposure: ¹/2sec @ f5.6

David Wilcock

With plenty of activity going on inside, Temple Mills East's 1958 power box, near Stratford in East London, is recorded on the night of 18th October 1985 and contrasts nicely with the Princes Risborough box opposite.
Camera: Nikon FM2, film rating: 300ASA
Exposure: 20secs @ f2.8

Brian Morrison

A superb sky as a backcloth to the scene, and at twilight on an August evening in 1985, the old 1905 GWR Princes Risborough signal box makes a picture in its own right.
Camera: Mamiya 645, film rating: 400ASA
Exposure: 1sec @ f5.6

Brian Beer

Kensington Olympia's 1892 LNWR South Main box is now the only one of three which currently survives here.
Camera: Mamiya 645, film rating: 400ASA
Exposure: 10secs @ f5.6

Brian Beer

Nightfall in the West Country

With an unpleasant West Country drizzle gently falling, the station lighting at Plymouth reflects in the platform and assists the overall illumination of the scene, as Class 47/4 No. 47466 arrives with the 10.30 service from Liverpool Lime Street on 21st February 1982.
Camera: Bronica EC, film rating: 400ASA
Exposure: 20secs @ f5.6

Brian Morrison

Just a few weeks before becoming an InterCity 125 HST working, the 14.37 Leeds-Plymouth train pauses at Teignmouth for the booked stop on 17th September 1981, powered by Class 45/0 'Peak' No. 45036.
Camera: Praktisix II, film rating: 400ASA
Exposure: 10secs @ f8

Geoff Gillham

Class 33/0 "Crompton" No. 33037, hauling the 19.30 Meldon Quarry-Salisbury stone train, is held on the old Exeter St Davids station centre road, on the night of 15th September 1982, awaiting departure of the Class 117 dmu set No. B439 on a local service for Exmouth.
Camera: Mamiya 645, film rating: 400ASA
Exposure: 10secs @ f5.6

Colin Marsden

With marker lights aglow, Class 25/2 No. 25220 stands at Newton Abbot station on 27th November 1976 heading the 20.00 Saturday local service for Paignton.
Camera: Minolta SRT101b, film rating: 200ASA
Exposure: 1min @ f11

Stephen Montgomery

The nameplate and badge on the side of "Crompton" No. 33025 *Sultan* are thrown into relief by the station lighting at Bath Spa on 3rd January 1982, as the driver awaits the guard's signal prior to restarting the 16.15 service from Portsmouth Harbour to Bristol Temple Meads. Following serious accident damage it was thought that this locomotive would have to be scrapped and the nameplates were therefore transferred to another of the class, No. 33114. However, it eventually transpired that 33025 was reprieved and has had its nameplates returned.
Camera: Praktisix II, film rating: 400ASA
Exposure: 15secs @ f8

Geoff Gillham

Docklands in the Dark

Two ends of the line on the Docklands Light Railway are illustrated here, with unit No. 08 (top) standing at Island Gardens station on 20th September 1988 with a service for Stratford in East London. (Below), the depot sidings at Poplar with units Nos 04, 11 and 10 awaiting their next morning's duties.

Camera: Canon EF, film rating: 400ASA
Exposure: 1sec @ f5.6 and 20secs @ f4

Both Ken Brunt

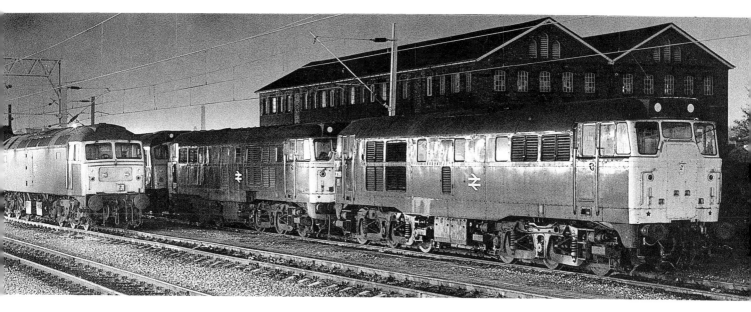

The Ubiquitous Class 31

▲
'Stabled' at Nuneaton overnight on 1st March 1984 are, from right to left, Class 31/1s Nos 31289 and 31247, Class 25/2 No. 25175 and Class 47/0 No. 47227. Lighting from the station platform provided satisfactory illumination for the latter locomotive but the leading Class 31/1, being further from the light source, required a 'fill-in' flash in order to register satisfactorily on the film.
Camera: Nikon FM2, film rating: 400ASA
Exposure: 30secs @ f2.8 + flash
Brian Morrison

►
As mentioned earlier, in the 1988/89 timetables, the 15.30 (FO) Derby-St Pancras InterCity service and 18.20 return was, surprisingly, booked to be hauled by a Class 37 but, in fact, this class of locomotive appeared on the trains on only a few occasions before being substituted by the more usual Class 47. On the second week of the timetable, however, a Class 31/4, No. 31438, was the substitute provided, as seen here at St Pancras on 14th October 1988 with the 18.20 to Derby. The station clock indicates that the train was running late.
Camera: Nikon FM2, film rating: 400ASA
Exposure: 1sec @ f2.8
Brian Morrison

▼ A northbound 'Speedlink' freight stops momentarily for an adverse signal on the station avoiding line at Peterborough on 18th August 1988 hauled by Class 31/1 No. 31248, which is painted in Railfreight Sector grey livery with wrap-around yellow ends.
Camera: Nikon FM2, film rating: 400ASA
Exposure: 20secs @ f5.6
Brian Morrison

Making good use of its newly fitted headlight, Class 31/4 No. 31455 pauses at Leeds station on 29th December 1984 with a Hull-Lancaster train. Rain is invariably unpleasant for the railway photographer but at night it can enhance a scene such as this, with the locomotive's marker lights reflecting in the platform puddle. In wet conditions, the camera can be protected from the elements by judicious use of a station canopy or even an umbrella.
Camera: Mamiya 645, film rating: 400ASA
Exposure: 20secs @ f8

Brian Beer

In pristine condition after its naming ceremony only the day before, Class 31/4 No. 31444 *Keighley and Worth Valley Railway* makes the required parcels pick-up at Peterborough station on 18th August 1988 with the 18.09 parcels train (1A37) from Leeds to King's Cross. To date, this locomotive is the only one of the class without a market light panel to receive a name.
Camera: Nikon FM2, film rating: 400ASA
Exposure: 8secs @ f4

Brian Morrison

Already some ten minutes behind time, the driver of eth fitted Class 31/4 No. 31423 impatiently looks back along his train at Nuneaton in order to ascertain how the parcels loading is progressing on the 18.18 Birmingham New Street-Norwich service on 1st March 1984.
Camera: Nikon FM2, film rating: 400ASA
Exposure: 2secs @ f2.8

Brian Morrison

Opposite:
With newly-fitted headlight not yet switched on, another Class 31/4, No. 31446, stands at Doncaster station on 7th November 1984 with the 21.00 train for Hull.
Camera: Nikon FM2, film rating: 400ASA
Exposure: 5secs @ f4

Colin Marsden

Salisbury After Sunset

Although the fine Southern Railway lattice-post upper quadrant signal stands 'off', the cab of Class 50 No. 50015 *Valiant* is empty as a crew change is awaited at Salisbury on the 18.20 Exeter St Davids-Waterloo service on 20th March 1981.
Camera: Praktisix II, film rating: 400ASA
Exposure: 10secs @ f11

Geoff Gillham

A brisk north wind sends clouds scudding across the moon as Class 31/4 No. 31401 waits at Salisbury on 4th September 1979 with the 17.15 train from Portsmouth Harbour to Bristol Temple Meads.
Camera: Praktisix II, film rating: 400ASA
Exposure: 8secs @ f8

Geoff Gillham

A fireworks display in a local park lights up the sky behind Salisbury station on Guy Fawkes night 1971, as Class 35 'Hymek' B-B No. D7001, fresh from overhaul ˙at Swindon Works, powers the 17.35 Bristol Temple Meads-Portsmouth Harbour train.
Camera: Yashica 124, film speed: 400ASA
Exposure: 20secs @ f8

Geoff Gillham

Shortly after being painted in lined GWR green and re-named *Sir Edward Elgar* from the original name of *Hercules*, Class 50 No. 50007 stands at Salisbury station's platform 2 on 30th March 1984 at the head of the 19.10 Waterloo-Exeter St Davids service. With the locomotive driver keeping a watchful eye, two youngsters snatch the opportunity of taking a rubbing of the new nameplate.
Camera: Praktisix II, film rating: 400ASA
Exposure: 10secs @ f8

Geoff Gillham

Bumps in the Night

On 25th August 1974, Class 47/0 No. 47236 was derailed at Dorchester West whilst hauling a return railwaymen's excursion from Weymouth to Hereford. Both the Bristol steam crane and the Eastleigh crane were called out to lift the recalcitrant "Duff" back onto the rails.
Camera and film rating: not known
Exposure: flash @ approx. f4

B.L. Jackson

The Eastleigh breakdown crane, hauled appropriately by "Crompton" No. 33008 *Eastleigh,* pauses at Salisbury on 1st September 1983 before continuing to the scene of an accident near Wylye, where a Bristol Temple Meads-Salisbury dmu had collided with a farm tractor on an unmanned crossing. Happily there were no injuries.
Camera: Praktisix II, film rating: 400ASA
Exposure: 15secs @ f8

Geoff Gillham

On 19th December 1973, an accident occurred on the Western main line at West Ealing involving the 17.18 Paddington-Oxford train hauled by Class 52 'Western' No. D1007 *Western Talisman* which had been derailed and thrown onto its side. Endeavouring to clear the line and reduce delays on the following morning is the Old Oak Common steam crane.
Camera: Yashica 124, film rating: 400ASA
Exposure: 1/60th sec @ f4.5 + flash

Colin Marsden

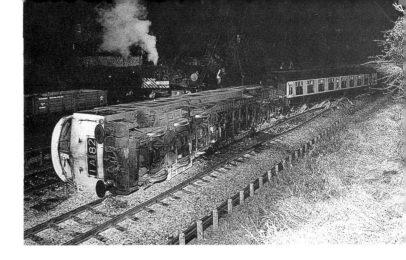

Following derailment of a cement train at Cupar, Fife, on 2nd June 1988, some 1,000yds of track were torn up and a road bridge destroyed, resulting in curtailment of normal services for over a week. In the small hours of 3rd June, Class 26/0 No. 26014 has hauled the breakdown train as far along the line as it could go while, in the distance, the Eastfield crane is already at work lifting some of the 'Presflo' wagons from trackside.
Camera: Nikon FM2, film rating: 400ASA
Exposure: 20secs @ f2.8 + flash

Brian Morrison

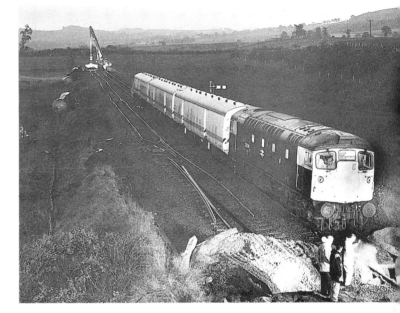

On 23rd December 1954 at Maybury, near Woking, a 4COR "Nelson" emu forming the 19.50 Waterloo-Portsmouth Harbour service was run into by a Class N15x 'Remembrance' 4-6-0 steam locomotive No. 32327 *Trevithick,* which was hauling the 19.54 Waterloo-Basingstoke train. Shortly following the incident, this photograph was taken by an unknown cameraman as the rescue services were carrying out their allotted tasks.
Camera and film rating: unknown
Exposure: approx. 1/10th sec @ f4.5 under floodlights

Colin Marsden collection

Wainwright's South Eastern & Chatham Railway Class H 0-4-4T No. 263 rolls into Horsted Keynes station, on the Bluebell Railway, on 17th October 1981 with a "Starlight Special" from Sheffield Park which included dining facilities.
Camera: Mamiya 645, film rating: 400ASA
Exposure: multiple flash during time exposure of 2mins @ f5.6

Colin Marsden

Stanier Class 8P 'Coronation' Pacific No.46229 *Duchess of Hamilton* raises steam at Carnforth on 11th November 1980 preparatory to taking out a rail tour.
Camera: Mamiya 645, film rating: 400ASA
Exposure: 45secs @ f11

David Wilcock

A 1939 Hudswell Clarke (No. 1709) 0-6-0ST *Slough Estates Ltd No.5* works the Yorkshire Dales Railway at Embsay Station in November 1980. Flash has 'frozen' the exhaust and steam giving an impression of movement, but the well-exposed carriage lights rather give the game away.
Camera: Mamiya 645, film rating: 400ASA
Exposure: 10secs @ f4 + flash

David Wilcock

The replica *Rocket* at London Heathrow Airfreight Terminal on 6th March 1983 is waiting to be loaded aboard Japan Air Lines "Jumbo" cargo aircraft No. JA8151, a part of which can be seen in the background, for exhibition and steaming at the Osaka Exhibition of that year. For all intents and purposes the locomotive was in darkness, and a flash gun was not being carried on this occasion as the original 'press call' was for daylight hours. The problem was solved by persuading the drivers of two vans and a car to turn their headlights onto *Rocket*, enabling a short hand-held exposure to be made, a tripod not being one of the anticipated accessories either!
Camera: Nikon FM2, film rating: 400ASA
Exposure: 1/30th sec @ f1.4

Brian Morrison

Hauling a Severn Valley Railway private charter train named "The Taysider", Gresley Class A4 Pacific No. 60009 *Union of South Africa* stops alongside the goods shed at Kirkcaldy, Fife, to take on water during the run from Mossend to Dundee and back via Stirling and Perth on 14th November 1981.
Camera: Mamiya 645, film rating: 400ASA
Exposure: 20secs @ f5.6

David Wilcock

Opposite:

The yard lighting at Steamtown Carnforth is good and enables excellent night scenes such as this to be produced. Backed by the ash-plant and sister "Black Five" No. 5407, Stanier Class 5MT No. 4767, sporting a Bank Hall 27A shed plate, raises steam in order to haul a "Cumbrian Mountain Express" special over the Settle & Carlisle route on the following day, 21st February 1981.
Camera: Mamiya 645, film rating: 400ASA
Exposure: 20secs @ f5.6

David Wilcock

With the ground covered in thick, powdery snow and in the bitterly cold conditions which prevailed for much of December 1981, Barclay (No. 2333) 0-4-0ST *David* steam heats the Lakeside & Haverthwaite Railway's Mk 1 stock in preparation for the following morning's "Father Christmas Specials".
Camera: Canon AE1, film rating: 400ASA
Exposure: 45secs @ f5.6

Nigel Harris

Just before dawn at Glenboig Colliery, near Coatbridge on Strathclyde, on a chilly October day in 1981, a very long haul of coal hoppers headed by a 1950 Barclay 0-4-0ST, No. 2296 waits beside the weighbridge hut for the crew to clock on. Less than two months later, the National Coal Board had closed down all operations here.
Camera: Mamiya 645, film rating: 400ASA
Exposure: 1min @ f5.6

David Wilcock

The last train of the day on the first day of 1981 has arrived at Horsted Keynes station and the Bulleid Class Q1 0-6-0 No. 33001, which has provided traction, sets back ready to return 'light engine' to Sheffield Park.
Camera: Maniya 645, film rating: 400ASA
Exposure: 30secs @ f11

David Wilcock

With LMS "Black Five" 4-6-0 No. 5407 piloting Southern 4-6-0 No. 850 *Lord Nelson* northwards from Hellifield on the return leg of the "Cumbrian Mountain Express" to Carnforth on 22nd November 1980, the photographer did not need to use his own flash gun, as the illumination provided by the many others with flash facilities who were gathered for the event was quite sufficient.

Camera: Mamiya 645, film rating: 400ASA
Exposure: 45secs @ f5.6 with flash from others' flash guns

David Wilcock

October 24th 1981 heralded the first appearance at Carnforth of the Gresley Class K1 Mogul No. 2005, when it was used from Newcastle in connection with a 15th anniversary special of the North Eastern Locomotive Preservation Group. This fine front end silhouette was produced by deliberately aiming the camera into the strong yard lights which were shining on the other side of the engine.

Camera: Mamiya 645, film rating: 400ASA
Exposure: 1sec @ f5.6

David Wilcock

In superb condition, the Bluebell Railway's 9000 Class "Dukedog" No. 3217 *Earl of Berkeley* is posed at the GWR Society's Didcot Railway Centre during the autumn of 1984 when it was there on loan.
Camera: Mamiya 645, film rating: 400ASA
Exposure: 30secs @ f5.6

Chris Lyons

On 12th July 1982, Lancashire & Yorkshire Railway 0-6-0 No. 1300 rests among the trees at Lakeside station during a pause in filming sequences for the production of 'Wagner' which starred the late Richard Burton. The engine was taken to the Lakeside & Haverthwaite Railway from its usual Carnforth home specially for the film, for which it was fitted with a powerful headlight in an attempt to try to give it a Continental appearance. It is the headlight which is providing most of the frontal illumination here, assisted by various lights used by the film crew.
Camera: Canon AE1, film rating: 400ASA
Exposure: 20secs @ f5.6

Nigel Harris

A fine study of the front end of Gresley Class A3 Pacific No. 4472 *Flying Scotsman* under the Carnforth yard lights. The reflections provided by the polished condition of the paintwork on the ever-growing fleet of preserved steam locomotives, greatly enhances a photograph such as this.
Camera: Canon AE1, film rating: 400ASA
Exposure: 15secs @ f5.6

Nigel Harris

Whilst piloting the "Great Western Limited" special from Bristol Temple Meads to Plymouth on 7th April 1985, 7800 Class 'Manor' 4-6-0 No. 7819 *Hinton Manor* failed at Exeter with a melted bearing on the right leading axle, and the train had to be taken on to its destination by a pair of Class 37 diesels. The 'Manor' was soon back in action, however, following an on-the-spot renewal of the offending part. With the repair completed, the locomotive travelled to Plymouth overnight in order to power the return journey of the train on the following day, which was accomplished without further hitch. In this view *Hinton Manor* is awaiting a path through Dawlish Warren station on its overnight journey to Plymouth.
Camera: Mamiya 645, film rating: 400ASA
Exposure: 15secs @ f8

David Nicholas

The end.

Camera: Nikon FM2, film rating: 400ASA
Exposure: 4secs @ f2.8
Brian Morrison